Books are to be returne
the last date b

CW01113140

Ubur

LIBREX-

Fultus™ *Books*

ubuntu
linux for human beings

Ubuntu 9.10
Ubuntu Installation Guide

ISBN-10: 1-59682-171-X
ISBN-13: 978-1-59682-171-2

Copyright © 2004-2009 the Debian Installer team

Copyright © 2004-2009 Canonical Ltd.

Cover design and book layout by Fultus Corporation

Published by Fultus Corporation

Publisher Web: *www.fultus.com*
Linbrary - Linux Library: *www.linbrary.com*
Online Bookstore: *store.fultus.com*
email: *production@fultus.com*

This material may only be distributed subject to the terms and conditions set forth in the Creative Commons ShareAlike 3.0 License (CC-BY-SA),
(the latest version is presently available at *http://creativecommons.org/licenses/by-sa/3.0/legalcode*).

Ubuntu, Canonical and Ubuntu logo are trademarks or registered trademarks of **Canonical Ltd.**, Inc., in the U.S. and other countries. All product names and services identified throughout this manual are trademarks or registered trademarks of their respective companies.

The author and publisher have made every effort in the preparation of this book to ensure the accuracy of the information. However, the information contained in this book is offered without warranty, either express or implied. Neither the author nor the publisher nor any dealer or distributor will be held liable for any damages caused or alleged to be caused either directly or indirectly by this book.

Table of Contents

List of Tables 10
Credits and License 11
Abstract 12
Installing Ubuntu 9.10 "Karmic Koala" For i386 13
Chapter 1. Welcome to Ubuntu 14
   1.1. What is Ubuntu? 14
      1.1.1. Sponsorship by Canonical 15
   1.2. What is Debian? 15
      1.2.1. Ubuntu and Debian 16
         1.2.1.1. Package selection 16
         1.2.1.2. Releases 17
         1.2.1.3. Development community 17
         1.2.1.4. Freedom and Philosophy 17
         1.2.1.5. Ubuntu and other Debian derivatives 18
   1.3. What is GNU/Linux? 18
   1.4. Getting Ubuntu 19
   1.5. Getting the Newest Version of This Document 20
   1.6. Organization of This Document 20
   1.7. About Copyrights and Software Licenses 21
Chapter 2. System Requirements 23
   2.1. Supported Hardware 23
      2.1.1. Supported Architectures 23
      2.1.2. CPU, Main Boards, and Video Support 24
         2.1.2.1. CPU 24
         2.1.2.2. I/O Bus 24
      2.1.3. Laptops 24
      2.1.4. Multiple Processors 25
      2.1.5. Graphics Card Support 25
      2.1.6. Network Connectivity Hardware 25
         2.1.6.1. Wireless Network Cards 25
      2.1.7. Peripherals and Other Hardware 26
   2.2. Devices Requiring Firmware 26

Ubuntu 9.10

2.3. Purchasing Hardware Specifically for GNU/Linux 26
   2.3.1. Avoid Proprietary or Closed Hardware 27
   2.3.2. Windows-specific Hardware 27
2.4. Installation Media 28
   2.4.1. CD-ROM/DVD-ROM 28
   2.4.2. Hard Disk 29
   2.4.3. USB Memory Stick 29
   2.4.4. Network 29
   2.4.5. Un*x or GNU system 29
   2.4.6. Supported Storage Systems 29
2.5. Memory and Disk Space Requirements 30

Chapter 3. Before Installing Ubuntu 31

3.1. Overview of the Installation Process 31
3.2. Back Up Your Existing Data! 32
3.3. Information You Will Need 33
   3.3.1. Documentation 33
      3.3.1.1. Installation Manual 33
      3.3.1.2. Hardware documentation 33
   3.3.2. Finding Sources of Hardware Information 33
   3.3.3. Hardware Compatibility 34
   3.3.4. Network Settings 35
3.4. Meeting Minimum Hardware Requirements 36
3.5. Pre-Partitioning for Multi-Boot Systems 37
   3.5.1. Partitioning From DOS or Windows 38
      3.5.1.1. Lossless Repartitioning When Starting From DOS, Win-32 or OS/2 39
      3.5.1.2. Partitioning for DOS 39
3.6. Pre-Installation Hardware and Operating System Setup 40
   3.6.1. Invoking the BIOS Set-Up Menu 40
   3.6.2. Boot Device Selection 41
      3.6.2.1. Changing the Boot Order on IDE Computers 41
      3.6.2.2. Changing the Boot Order on SCSI Computers 42
   3.6.3. Miscellaneous BIOS Settings 42
      3.6.3.1. CD-ROM Settings 42
      3.6.3.2. Extended vs. Expanded Memory 42
      3.6.3.3. Virus Protection 42
      3.6.3.4. Shadow RAM 42
      3.6.3.5. Memory Hole 43
      3.6.3.6. Advanced Power Management 43

3.6.4. Hardware Issues to Watch Out For	43
Chapter 4. Obtaining System Installation Media	**44**
4.1. Official Ubuntu CD-ROMs	44
4.2. Downloading Files from Ubuntu Mirrors	44
4.2.1. Where to Find Installation Images	45
4.3. Preparing Files for USB Memory Stick Booting	45
4.3.1. Copying the files — the easy way	46
4.3.2. Copying the files — the flexible way	46
4.3.2.1. Partitioning the USB stick	46
4.3.2.2. Adding the installer image	47
4.3.3. Booting the USB stick	47
4.4. Preparing Files for Hard Disk Booting	47
4.4.1. Hard disk installer booting using LILO or GRUB	48
4.5. Preparing Files for TFTP Net Booting	48
4.5.1. Setting up a BOOTP server	49
4.5.2. Setting up a DHCP server	49
4.5.2.1. Enabling PXE Booting in the DHCP configuration	50
4.5.3. Enabling the TFTP Server	51
4.5.4. Move TFTP Images Into Place	51
4.6. Automatic Installation	51
4.6.1. Automatic Installation Using the Ubuntu Installer	52
4.6.2. Automatic Installation Using Kickstart	52
4.6.2.1. Additions	53
4.6.2.2. Missing features	53
Chapter 5. Booting the Installation System	**55**
5.1. Booting the Installer on Intel x86	55
5.1.1. Booting from a CD-ROM	55
5.1.2. Booting from Linux Using LILO or GRUB	55
5.1.3. Booting from USB Memory Stick	56
5.1.4. Booting with TFTP	56
5.1.4.1. NIC or Motherboard that support PXE	57
5.1.4.2. NIC with Network BootROM	57
5.1.4.3. Etherboot	57
5.1.5. The Boot Screen	57
5.2. Boot Parameters	58
5.2.1. Ubuntu Installer Parameters	59
5.2.1.1. Using boot parameters to answer questions	63
5.2.1.2. Passing parameters to kernel modules	64

5.2.1.3. Blacklisting kernel modules 64
5.3. Troubleshooting the Installation Process..65
 5.3.1. CD-ROM Reliability 65
  5.3.1.1. Common issues 65
  5.3.1.2. How to investigate and maybe solve issues 65
 5.3.2. Boot Configuration..67
 5.3.3. Common Intel x86 Installation Problems...67
  5.3.3.1. System Freeze During the PCMCIA Configuration Phase 68
  5.3.3.2. System Freeze while Loading USB Modules 68
 5.3.4. Interpreting the Kernel Startup Messages 68
 5.3.5. Reporting Installation Problems..69
 5.3.6. Submitting Installation Reports...69
Chapter 6. Using the Ubuntu Installer..71
 6.1. How the Installer Works 71
 6.2. Components Introduction 72
 6.3. Using Individual Components...75
  6.3.1. Setting up Ubuntu Installer and Hardware Configuration........................75
   6.3.1.1. Check available memory / low memory mode 75
   6.3.1.2. Selecting Localization Options...76
   6.3.1.3. Choosing a Keyboard 77
   6.3.1.4. Looking for the Ubuntu Installer ISO Image 77
   6.3.1.5. Configuring the Network 78
   6.3.1.6. Configuring the Clock 79
  6.3.2. Partitioning and Mount Point Selection..79
   6.3.2.1. Guided Partitioning..79
   6.3.2.2. Manual Partitioning...81
   6.3.2.3. Configuring Multidisk Devices (Software RAID)....................82
   6.3.2.4. Configuring the Logical Volume Manager (LVM)....................86
   6.3.2.5. Configuring Encrypted Volumes...87
  6.3.3. Installing the Base System 91
  6.3.4. Setting Up Users And Passwords 91
   6.3.4.1. Create an Ordinary User...92
  6.3.5. Installing Additional Software..92
   6.3.5.1. Configuring apt 92
    6.3.5.1.1   Installing from more than one CD or DVD...............93
    6.3.5.1.2   Using a network mirror 94
   6.3.5.2. Selecting and Installing Software 95
  6.3.6. Making Your System Bootable 96

Installation Guide

- 6.3.6.1. Detecting other operating systems ... 96
- 6.3.6.2. Install the Grub Boot Loader on a Hard Disk ... 97
- 6.3.6.3. Install the LILO Boot Loader on a Hard Disk ... 97
- 6.3.6.4. Continue Without Boot Loader ... 98
- 6.3.7. Finishing the Installation ... 98
  - 6.3.7.1. Setting the System Clock ... 98
  - 6.3.7.2. Reboot the System ... 98
- 6.3.8. Miscellaneous ... 98
  - 6.3.8.1. Saving the installation logs ... 99
  - 6.3.8.2. Using the Shell and Viewing the Logs ... 99
  - 6.3.8.3. Installation Over the Network ... 100
- 6.4. Loading Missing Firmware ... 101
  - 6.4.1. Preparing a medium ... 102
  - 6.4.2. Firmware and the Installed System ... 103

Chapter 7. Booting Into Your New Ubuntu System ... 104
- 7.1. The Moment of Truth ... 104
- 7.2. Mounting encrypted volumes ... 104
  - 7.2.1. dm-crypt ... 104
  - 7.2.2. loop-AES ... 105
  - 7.2.3. Troubleshooting ... 105
- 7.3. Log In ... 106

Chapter 8. Next Steps and Where to Go From Here ... 108
- 8.1. Shutting down the system ... 108
- 8.2. If You Are New to Unix ... 108
- 8.3. Orienting Yourself to Ubuntu ... 108
  - 8.3.1. Ubuntu Packaging System ... 109
  - 8.3.2. Application Version Management ... 109
  - 8.3.3. Cron Job Management ... 109
- 8.4. Further Reading and Information ... 110
- 8.5. Setting Up Your System To Use E-Mail ... 110
  - 8.5.1. Default E-Mail Configuration ... 111
  - 8.5.2. Sending E-Mails Outside The System ... 111
  - 8.5.3. Configuring the Exim4 Mail Transport Agent ... 112
- 8.6. Compiling a New Kernel ... 113
  - 8.6.1. Kernel Image Management ... 114
- 8.7. Recovering a Broken System ... 115

Appendix A. Installation Howto ... 117
- A.1. Booting the installer ... 117
  - A.1.1. CDROM ... 117

    A.1.2. USB memory stick 117
    A.1.3. Booting from network..118
  A.2. Installation 118
  A.3. And finally… 119
Appendix B. Automating the installation using preseeding..120
  B.1. Introduction 120
    B.1.1. Preseeding methods 120
    B.1.2. Limitations 121
  B.2. Using preseeding 121
    B.2.1. Loading the preconfiguration file 121
    B.2.2. Using boot parameters to preseed questions..122
    B.2.3. Auto mode..123
    B.2.4. Aliases useful with preseeding...125
    B.2.5. Using a DHCP server to specify preconfiguration files 126
  B.3. Creating a preconfiguration file 126
  B.4. Contents of the preconfiguration file (for jaunty) 127
    B.4.1. Localization 127
    B.4.2. Network configuration 128
    B.4.3. Mirror settings 130
    B.4.4. Clock and time zone setup 130
    B.4.5. Partitioning...131
    B.4.6. Partitioning using RAID..132
    B.4.7. Controlling how partitions are mounted 133
    B.4.8. Base system installation...134
    B.4.9. Account setup 134
    B.4.10. Apt setup 135
    B.4.11. Package selection 136
    B.4.12. Boot loader installation..137
    B.4.13. Finishing up the installation 138
    B.4.14. X configuration 138
    B.4.15. Preseeding other packages 138
  B.5. Advanced options 139
    B.5.1. Running custom commands during the installation 139
    B.5.2. Using preseeding to change default values 139
    B.5.3. Chainloading preconfiguration files..140
Appendix C. Partitioning for Ubuntu 141
  C.1. Deciding on Ubuntu Partitions and Sizes 141
  C.2. The Directory Tree 142
  C.3. Recommended Partitioning Scheme 143

- C.4. Device Names in Linux..144
- C.5. Ubuntu Partitioning Programs 145
  - C.5.1. Partitioning for Intel x86 146

Appendix D. Random Bits..148
- D.1. Linux Devices...148
  - D.1.1. Setting Up Your Mouse 149
- D.2. Disk Space Needed for Tasks...150
- D.3. Disk Space Needed...151
- D.4. Installing Ubuntu from a Unix/Linux System 151
  - D.4.1. Getting Started 151
  - D.4.2. Install debootstrap 152
  - D.4.3. Run debootstrap...152
  - D.4.4. Configure The Base System 153
    - D.4.4.1. Create device files 153
    - D.4.4.2. Mount Partitions 153
    - D.4.4.3. Setting Timezone...154
    - D.4.4.4. Configure Networking..154
    - D.4.4.5. Configure Apt..156
    - D.4.4.6. Configure Locales and Keyboard..156
  - D.4.5. Install a Kernel...156
  - D.4.6. Set up the Boot Loader 157
  - D.4.7. Finishing touches 158
  - D.4.8. Create a User...158
  - D.4.9. Install the Ubuntu Desktop 158
- D.5. Installing Ubuntu over Parallel Line IP (PLIP) 159
  - D.5.1. Requirements...159
  - D.5.2. Setting up source...159
  - D.5.3. Installing target 160
- D.6. Installing Ubuntu using PPP over Ethernet (PPPoE) 161
- D.7. The Graphical Installer 162
  - D.7.1. Using the graphical installer 163
  - D.7.2. Known issues 163

Appendix E. Administrivia..164
- E.1. About This Document..164
- E.2. Contributing to This Document 164
- E.3. Major Contributions 165
- E.4. Trademark Acknowledgement...165

Appendix F. GNU General Public License 166

Ubuntu 9.10 Official Documentation Collection 173

List of Tables

Table 3.1. Hardware Information Needed for an Install 34
Table 3.2. Recommended Minimum System Requirements 36

Credits and License

This manual is free software; you may redistribute it and/or modify it under the terms of the GNU General Public License. Please refer to the license in *Appendix F, GNU General Public License*.

Abstract

This document contains installation instructions for the Ubuntu 9.10 system (codename "Karmic Koala"), for the Intel x86 ("i386") architecture. It also contains pointers to more information and information on how to make the most of your new Ubuntu system.

Installing Ubuntu 9.10 "Karmic Koala" For i386

We are delighted that you have decided to try Ubuntu, and are sure that you will find that Ubuntu's GNU/Linux distribution is unique. Ubuntu brings together high-quality free software from around the world, integrating it into a coherent whole. We believe that you will find that the result is truly more than the sum of the parts.

We understand that many of you want to install Ubuntu without reading this manual, and the Ubuntu installer is designed to make this possible. If you don't have time to read the whole Installation Guide right now, we recommend that you read the Installation Howto, which will walk you through the basic installation process, and links to the manual for more advanced topics or for when things go wrong. The Installation Howto can be found in *Appendix A, Installation Howto*.

With that said, we hope that you have the time to read most of this manual, and doing so will lead to a more informed and likely more successful installation experience.

Chapter 1.
Welcome to Ubuntu

This chapter provides an overview of the Ubuntu Project, and the Debian Project upon which it is based. If you already know about the Ubuntu Project's history and the Ubuntu distribution, feel free to skip to the next chapter.

1.1. What is Ubuntu?

Ubuntu is a complete desktop Linux operating system, freely available with both community and professional support. The Ubuntu community is built on the ideas enshrined in the Ubuntu Manifesto: that software should be available free of charge, that software tools should be usable by people in their local language and despite any disabilities, and that people should have the freedom to customize and alter their software in whatever way they see fit.

- *Ubuntu will always be free of charge*, and there is no extra fee for the "enterprise edition", we make our very best work available to everyone on the same Free terms.
- Ubuntu includes the *very best in translations and accessibility infrastructure* that the Free Software community has to offer, to make Ubuntu usable by as many people as possible.
- Ubuntu is shipped in stable and regular release cycles; *a new release will be shipped every six months*. You can use the current stable release or the current development release. A release will be supported for 18 months.
- Ubuntu is entirely committed to the principles of open source software development; we encourage people to use open source software, improve it and pass it on.

Ubuntu is suitable for both desktop and server use. The current Ubuntu release supports Intel x86 (IBM-compatible PC), AMD64 (Hammer) and PowerPC (Apple iBook and Powerbook, G4 and G5) architectures.

Ubuntu includes more than 1000 pieces of software, starting with the Linux kernel version 2.6 and GNOME 2.26, and covering every standard desktop application from word processing and spreadsheet applications to internet access applications, web server software, email software, programming languages and tools and of course several games.

Installation Guide

1.1.1. Sponsorship by Canonical

The Ubuntu Project is sponsored by *Canonical Ltd.*[1] Canonical will not charge licence fees for Ubuntu, now or at any stage in the future. Canonical's business model is to provide technical support and professional services related to Ubuntu. We encourage more companies also to offer support for Ubuntu, and will list those that do on the Support pages of this web site.

1.2. What is Debian?

Debian is an all-volunteer organization dedicated to developing free software and promoting the ideals of the Free Software community. The Debian Project began in 1993, when Ian Murdock issued an open invitation to software developers to contribute to a complete and coherent software distribution based on the relatively new Linux kernel. That relatively small band of dedicated enthusiasts, originally funded by the *Free Software Foundation*[2] and influenced by the *GNU*[3] philosophy, has grown over the years into an organization of around 1000 *Debian Developers*.

Debian Developers are involved in a variety of activities, including *Web*[4] and *FTP*[5] site administration, graphic design, legal analysis of software licenses, writing documentation, and, of course, maintaining software packages.

In the interest of communicating our philosophy and attracting developers who believe in the principles that Debian stands for, the Debian Project has published a number of documents that outline our values and serve as guides to what it means to be a Debian Developer:

- The *Debian Social Contract*[6] is a statement of Debian's commitments to the Free Software Community. Anyone who agrees to abide to the Social Contract may become a *maintainer*[7]. Any maintainer can introduce new software into Debian — provided that the software meets our criteria for being free, and the package follows our quality standards.
- The *Debian Free Software Guidelines*[8] are a clear and concise statement of Debian's criteria for free software. The DFSG is a very influential document in the Free Software Movement, and was the foundation of the *The Open Source Definition*[9].

---

[1] *http://www.canonical.com/*

[2] *http://www.fsf.org/*

[3] *http://www.gnu.org/gnu/the-gnu-project.html*

[4] *http://www.debian.org/*

[5] *ftp://ftp.debian.org/*

[6] *http://www.debian.org/social_contract*

[7] *http://www.debian.org/doc/maint-guide/*

[8] *http://www.debian.org/social_contract#guidelines*

- The *Debian Policy Manual*[10] is an extensive specification of the Debian Project's standards of quality.

Debian developers are also involved in a number of other projects; some specific to Debian, others involving some or all of the Linux community. Some examples include:

- The *Linux Standard Base*[11] (LSB) is a project aimed at standardizing the basic GNU/Linux system, which will enable third-party software and hardware developers to easily design programs and device drivers for Linux-in-general, rather than for a specific GNU/Linux distribution.
- The *Filesystem Hierarchy Standard*[12] (FHS) is an effort to standardize the layout of the Linux file system. The FHS will allow software developers to concentrate their efforts on designing programs, without having to worry about how the package will be installed in different GNU/Linux distributions.
- *Debian Jr.*[13] is an internal project, aimed at making sure Debian has something to offer to our youngest users.

For more general information about Debian, see the *Debian FAQ*[14].

1.2.1. Ubuntu and Debian

Ubuntu and Debian are distinct but parallel and closely linked systems. The Ubuntu project seeks to complement the Debian project in the following areas:

1.2.1.1. Package selection

Ubuntu does not provide security updates and professional support for every package available in the open source world, but selects a complete set of packages making up a solid and comprehensive desktop system and provides support for that set of packages.

For users that want access to every known package, Ubuntu provides a "universe" component (set of packages) where users of Ubuntu systems install the latest version of any package that is not in the supported set. Most of the packages in Ubuntu universe are also in Debian, although there are other sources for universe too. See the Ubuntu Components page for more detail on the structure of the Ubuntu web distribution.

---

[9] *http://opensource.org/docs/definition_plain.html*
[10] *http://www.debian.org/doc/debian-policy/*
[11] *http://www.linuxbase.org/*
[12] *http://www.pathname.com/fhs/*
[13] *http://www.debian.org/devel/debian-jr/*
[14] *http://www.debian.org/doc/FAQ/*

1.2.1.2. Releases

Ubuntu makes a release every six months, and supports those releases for 18 months with daily security fixes and patches to critical bugs.

As Ubuntu prepares for release, we "freeze" a snapshot of Debian's development archive ("sid"). We start from "sid" in order to give ourselves the freedom to make our own decisions with regard to release management, independent of Debian's release-in-preparation. This is necessary because our release criteria are very different from Debian's.

As a simple example, a package might be excluded from Debian "testing" due to a build failure on any of the 11 architectures supported by Debian "sarge", but it is still suitable for Ubuntu if it builds and works on only three of them. A package will also be prevented from entering Debian "testing" if it has release-critical bugs according to Debian criteria, but a bug which is release-critical for Debian may not be as important for Ubuntu.

As a community, we choose places to diverge from Debian in ways that minimize the difference between Debian and Ubuntu. For example, we usually choose to update to the very latest version of Gnome rather than the older version in Debian, and we might do the same for key other pieces of infrastructure such as X or GCC. Those decisions are listed as Feature Goals for that release, and we work as a community to make sure that they are in place before the release happens.

1.2.1.3. Development community

Many Ubuntu developers are also recognized members of the Debian community. They continue to stay active in contributing to Debian both in the course of their work on Ubuntu and directly in Debian.

When Ubuntu developers fix bugs that are also present in Debian packages -- and since the projects are linked, this happens often -- they send their bugfixes to the Debian developers responsible for that package in Debian and record the patch URL in the Debian bug system. The long term goal of that work is to ensure that patches made by the full-time Ubuntu team members are immediately also included in Debian packages where the Debian maintainer likes the work.

In Ubuntu, team members can make a change to any package, even if it is one maintained by someone else. Once you are an Ubuntu maintainer it's encouraged that you fix problems you encounter, although we also encourage polite discussions between people with an interest in a given package to improve cooperation and reduce friction between maintainers.

1.2.1.4. Freedom and Philosophy

Debian and Ubuntu are grounded on the same free software philosophy. Both groups are explicitly committed to building an operating system of free software.

Differences between the groups lie in their treatment of non-computer applications (like documentation, fonts and binary firmware) and non-free software. Debian distributes a small amount of non-free software from their Internet servers. Ubuntu will also distribute binary drivers in the "restricted" component on its Internet servers but will not distribute any other software applications that do not meet its own Ubuntu Licensing Guidelines.

1.2.1.5. Ubuntu and other Debian derivatives

There are many other distributions that also share the same basic infrastructure (package and archive format). Ubuntu is distinguished from them in a number of ways.

First, Ubuntu contributes patches directly to Debian as bugs are fixed during the Ubuntu release process, not just when the release is actually made. With other Debian-style distributions, the source code and patches are made available in a "big bang" at release time, which makes them difficult to integrate into the upstream HEAD.

Second, Ubuntu includes a number of full-time contributors who are also Debian developers. Many of the other distributions that use Debian-style packaging do not include any active Debian contributors.

Third, Ubuntu makes much more frequent and fresher releases. Our release policy of releasing every six months is (at the time of writing :-) unique in the Linux distribution world. Ubuntu aims to provide you with a regular stable and security-supported snapshot of the best of the open source world.

1.3. What is GNU/Linux?

Linux is an operating system: a series of programs that let you interact with your computer and run other programs.

An operating system consists of various fundamental programs which are needed by your computer so that it can communicate and receive instructions from users; read and write data to hard disks, tapes, and printers; control the use of memory; and run other software. The most important part of an operating system is the kernel. In a GNU/Linux system, Linux is the kernel component. The rest of the system consists of other programs, many of which were written by or for the GNU Project. Because the Linux kernel alone does not form a working operating system, we prefer to use the term "GNU/Linux" to refer to systems that many people casually refer to as "Linux".

Linux is modelled on the Unix operating system. From the start, Linux was designed to be a multi-tasking, multi-user system. These facts are enough to make Linux different from other well-known operating systems. However, Linux is even more different than you might imagine. In contrast to other operating systems, nobody owns Linux. Much of its development is done by unpaid volunteers.

Development of what later became GNU/Linux began in 1984, when the *Free Software Foundation*[15] began development of a free Unix-like operating system called GNU.

The *GNU Project*[16] has developed a comprehensive set of free software tools for use with Unix™ and Unix-like operating systems such as Linux. These tools enable users to perform tasks ranging from the mundane (such as copying or removing files from the system) to the arcane (such as writing and compiling programs or doing sophisticated editing in a variety of document formats).

While many groups and individuals have contributed to Linux, the largest single contributor is still the Free Software Foundation, which created not only most of the tools used in Linux, but also the philosophy and the community that made Linux possible.

The *Linux kernel*[17] first appeared in 1991, when a Finnish computing science student named Linus Torvalds announced an early version of a replacement kernel for Minix to the Usenet newsgroup `comp.os.minix`. See Linux International's *Linux History Page*[18].

Linus Torvalds continues to coordinate the work of several hundred developers with the help of a few trusty deputies. Information about the `linux-kernel` mailing list can be found on the *linux-kernel mailing list FAQ*[19].

Linux users have immense freedom of choice in their software. For example, Linux users can choose from a dozen different command line shells and several graphical desktops. This selection is often bewildering to users of other operating systems, who are not used to thinking of the command line or desktop as something that they can change.

Linux is also less likely to crash, better able to run more than one program at the same time, and more secure than many operating systems. With these advantages, Linux is the fastest growing operating system in the server market. More recently, Linux has begun to be popular among home and business users as well.

1.4. Getting Ubuntu

For information on how to download Ubuntu from the Internet, see the *download web page*[20]. The *list of Ubuntu mirrors*[21] contains a full set of official Ubuntu mirrors, so you can easily find the nearest one.

Ubuntu can be upgraded after installation very easily. The installation procedure will help set up the system so that you can make those upgrades once installation is complete, if need be.

---

[15] *http://www.fsf.org/*
[16] *http://www.gnu.org/*
[17] *http://www.kernel.org/*
[18] *http://www.cs.cmu.edu/~awb/linux.history.html*
[19] *http://www.tux.org/lkml/*
[20] *http://www.ubuntu.com/download/*
[21] *http://wiki.ubuntu.com/Archive*

1.5. Getting the Newest Version of This Document

This document is constantly being revised. Updated versions of this installation manual are available from the *official Install Manual pages*[22].

1.6. Organization of This Document

This document is meant to serve as a manual for first-time Ubuntu users. It tries to make as few assumptions as possible about your level of expertise. However, we do assume that you have a general understanding of how the hardware in your computer works.

Expert users may also find interesting reference information in this document, including minimum installation sizes, details about the hardware supported by the Ubuntu installation system, and so on. We encourage expert users to jump around in the document.

In general, this manual is arranged in a linear fashion, walking you through the installation process from start to finish. Here are the steps in installing Ubuntu, and the sections of this document which correlate with each step:

1. Determine whether your hardware meets the requirements for using the installation system, in *Chapter 2, System Requirements*.
2. Backup your system, perform any necessary planning and hardware configuration prior to installing Ubuntu, in *Chapter 3, Before Installing Ubuntu*. If you are preparing a multi-boot system, you may need to create partitionable space on your hard disk for Ubuntu to use.
3. In *Chapter 4, Obtaining System Installation Media*, you will obtain the necessary installation files for your method of installation.
4. *Chapter 5, Booting the Installation System* describes booting into the installation system. This chapter also discusses troubleshooting procedures in case you have problems with this step.
5. Perform the actual installation according to *Chapter 6, Using the Ubuntu Installer*. This involves choosing your language, configuring peripheral driver modules, configuring your network connection, so that remaining installation files can be obtained directly from an Ubuntu server (if you are not installing from a CD), partitioning your hard drives and installation of a base system, then selection and installation of tasks. (Some background about setting up the partitions for your Ubuntu system is explained in *Appendix C, Partitioning for Ubuntu*.)
6. Boot into your newly installed base system, from *Chapter 7, Booting Into Your New Ubuntu System*.

---

[22] *http://help.ubuntu.com/9.10/installation-guide/i386/*

Installation Guide

Once you've got your system installed, you can read *Chapter 8, Next Steps and Where to Go From Here*. That chapter explains where to look to find more information about Unix and Ubuntu, and how to replace your kernel.

Finally, information about this document and how to contribute to it may be found in *Appendix E, Administrivia*.

1.7. About Copyrights and Software Licenses

We're sure that you've read some of the licenses that come with most commercial software — they usually say that you can only use one copy of the software on a single computer. This system's license isn't like that at all. We encourage you to put a copy of Debian GNU/Linux on every computer in your school or place of business. Lend your installation media to your friends and help them install it on their computers! You can even make thousands of copies and *sell* them — albeit with a few restrictions. Your freedom to install and use the system comes directly from Ubuntu being based on *free software*.

Calling software *free* doesn't mean that the software isn't copyrighted, and it doesn't mean that CDs containing that software must be distributed at no charge. Free software, in part, means that the licenses of individual programs do not require you to pay for the privilege of distributing or using those programs. Free software also means that not only may anyone extend, adapt, and modify the software, but that they may distribute the results of their work as well.

> **Note**
>
> The Ubuntu project, as a pragmatic concession to its users, does make some packages available that do not meet our criteria for being free. These packages are not part of the official distribution, however, and are only available from the `multiverse` area of Ubuntu mirrors; see the *Ubuntu web site*[23] for more information about the layout and contents of the archives.

Many of the programs in the system are licensed under the *GNU General Public License*, often simply referred to as "the GPL". The GPL requires you to make the *source code* of the programs available whenever you distribute a binary copy of the program; that provision of the license ensures that any user will be able to modify the software. Because of this provision, the source code[24] for all such programs is available in the Ubuntu system.

---

[23] http://www.ubuntu.com/ubuntu/components
[24] For information on how to locate, unpack, and build binaries from Ubuntu source packages, see the *Debian FAQ* (http://www.debian.org/doc/FAQ/), under "Basics of the Debian Package Management System".

21

Ubuntu 9.10

There are several other forms of copyright statements and software licenses used on the programs in Ubuntu. You can find the copyrights and licenses for every package installed on your system by looking in the file `/usr/share/doc/`*package-name*`/copyright` once you've installed a package on your system.

For more information about licenses and how Ubuntu determines whether software is free enough to be included in the main distribution, see the *Ubuntu License Policy*[25].

The most important legal notice is that this software comes with *no warranties*. The programmers who have created this software have done so for the benefit of the community. No guarantee is made as to the suitability of the software for any given purpose. However, since the software is free, you are empowered to modify that software to suit your needs — and to enjoy the benefits of the changes made by others who have extended the software in this way.

---

[25] *http://www.ubuntu.com/ubuntu/licensing*

Chapter 2.
System Requirements

This section contains information about what hardware you need to get started with Ubuntu. You will also find links to further information about hardware supported by GNU and Linux.

2.1. Supported Hardware

Ubuntu does not impose hardware requirements beyond the requirements of the Linux kernel and the GNU tool-sets. Therefore, any architecture or platform to which the Linux kernel, libc, **gcc**, etc. have been ported, and for which an Ubuntu port exists, can run Ubuntu.

Rather than attempting to describe all the different hardware configurations which are supported for Intel x86, this section contains general information and pointers to where additional information can be found.

2.1.1. Supported Architectures

Ubuntu 9.10 supports three major architectures and several variations of each architecture known as "flavors". Three other architectures (HP PA-RISC, Intel ia64, and IBM/Motorola PowerPC) have unofficial ports.

Architecture	Ubuntu Designation	Subarchitecture	Flavor
Intel x86-based	i386		
AMD64 & Intel EM64T	amd64		
HP PA-RISC	hppa	PA-RISC 1.1	32
		PA-RISC 2.0	64
Intel IA-64	ia64		
IBM/Motorola PowerPC	powerpc	PowerMac	pmac
Sun SPARC	sparc	sun4u	sparc64

Ubuntu 9.10

2.1.2. CPU, Main Boards, and Video Support

Complete information concerning supported peripherals can be found at *Linux Hardware Compatibility HOWTO*[1]. This section merely outlines the basics.

2.1.2.1. CPU

Nearly all x86-based (IA-32) processors still in use in personal computers are supported, including all varieties of Intel's "Pentium" series. This also includes 32-bit AMD and VIA (former Cyrix) processors, and processors like the Athlon XP and Intel P4 Xeon.

However, Debian GNU/Linux jaunty will *not* run on 386 or earlier processors. Despite the architecture name "i386", support for actual 80386 processors (and their clones) was dropped with the Sarge (r3.1) release of Debian[2]. (No version of Linux has ever supported the 286 or earlier chips in the series.) All i486 and later processors are still supported[3].

> **Note**
>
> If your system has a 64-bit processor from the AMD64 or Intel EM64T families, you will probably want to use the installer for the amd64 architecture instead of the installer for the (32-bit) i386 architecture.

2.1.2.2. I/O Bus

The system bus is the part of the motherboard which allows the CPU to communicate with peripherals such as storage devices. Your computer must use the ISA, EISA, PCI, PCIe, or VESA Local Bus (VLB, sometimes called the VL bus). Essentially all personal computers sold in recent years use one of these.

2.1.3. Laptops

Laptops are also supported and nowadays most laptops work out of the box. In case a laptop contains specialized or proprietary hardware, some specific functions may not be supported. To see if your particular laptop works well with GNU/Linux, see for example the *Linux Laptop pages*[4].

---

[1] *http://www.tldp.org/HOWTO/Hardware-HOWTO.html*

[2] We have long tried to avoid this, but in the end it was necessary due a unfortunate series of issues with the compiler and the kernel, starting with an bug in the C++ ABI provided by GCC. You should still be able to run Debian GNU/Linux on actual 80386 processors if you compile your own kernel and compile all packages from source, but that is beyond the scope of this manual.

[3] Many Debian packages will actually run slightly faster on modern computers as a positive side effect of dropping support for these old chips. The i486, introduced in 1989, has three opcodes (bswap, cmpxchg, and xadd) which the i386, introduced in 1986, did not have. Previously, these could not be easily used by most Debian packages; now they can.

[4] *http://www.linux-laptop.net/*

24

Installation Guide

2.1.4. Multiple Processors

Multiprocessor support — also called "symmetric multiprocessing" or SMP — is available for this architecture. The standard Ubuntu 9.10 kernel image has been compiled with *SMP-alternatives* support. This means that the kernel will detect the number of processors (or processor cores) and will automatically deactivate SMP on uniprocessor systems.

The 486 flavour of the Ubuntu kernel image packages for Intel x86 is not compiled with SMP support.

2.1.5. Graphics Card Support

You should be using a VGA-compatible display interface for the console terminal. Nearly every modern display card is compatible with VGA. Ancient standards such CGA, MDA, or HGA should also work, assuming you do not require X11 support. Note that X11 is not used during the installation process described in this document.

Ubuntu's support for graphical interfaces is determined by the underlying support found in X.Org's X11 system. Most AGP, PCI and PCIe video cards work under X.Org. Details on supported graphics buses, cards, monitors, and pointing devices can be found at *http://xorg.freedesktop.org/*. Ubuntu 9.10 ships with X.Org version 7.3.

2.1.6. Network Connectivity Hardware

Almost any network interface card (NIC) supported by the Linux kernel should also be supported by the installation system; modular drivers should normally be loaded automatically. This includes most PCI and PCMCIA cards. Many older ISA cards are supported as well.

ISDN is supported, but not during the installation.

2.1.6.1. Wireless Network Cards

Wireless networking is in general supported as well and a growing number of wireless adapters is supported by the official Linux kernel, although many of them do require firmware to be loaded. Wireless NICs that are not supported by the official Linux kernel can generally be made to work under Debian GNU/Linux, but are not supported during the installation.

The use of wireless networking during installation is still under development and whether it will work depends on the type of adaptor and the configuration of your wireless access point. If there is no other NIC you can use during the installation, it is still possible to install Debian GNU/Linux using a full CD-ROM or DVD image. Select the option to not configure a network and install using only the packages available from the CD/DVD. You can then install the driver and firmware you need after the installation is completed (after the reboot) and configure your network manually.

In some cases the driver you need may not be available as a Debian package. You will then have to look if there is source code available in the internet and compile the driver yourself. How to do this is outside the scope of this manual. If no Linux driver is available, your last resort is to use the `ndiswrapper` package, which allows you to use a Windows driver.

2.1.7. Peripherals and Other Hardware

Linux supports a large variety of hardware devices such as mice, printers, scanners, PCMCIA and USB devices. However, most of these devices are not required while installing the system.

USB hardware generally works fine, only some USB keyboards may require additional configuration (see *the section called "Hardware Issues to Watch Out For"*).

Again, see the *Linux Hardware Compatibility HOWTO*[5] to determine whether your specific hardware is supported by Linux.

2.2. Devices Requiring Firmware

Besides the availability of a device driver, some hardware also requires so-called *firmware* or *microcode* to be loaded into the device before it can become operational. This is most common for network interface cards (especially wireless NICs), but for example some USB devices and even some hard disk controllers also require firmware.

In most cases firmware is non-free according to the criteria used by the Debian GNU/Linux project and thus cannot be included in the main distribution or in the installation system. If the device driver itself is included in the distribution and if Debian GNU/Linux legally can distribute the firmware, it will often be available as a separate package from the non-free section of the archive.

However, this does not mean that such hardware cannot be used during an installation. Starting with Debian GNU/Linux 5.0, `debian-installer` supports loading firmware files or packages containing firmware from a removable medium, such as a floppy disk or USB stick. See *the section called "Loading Missing Firmware"* for detailed information on how to load firmware files or packages during the installation.

2.3. Purchasing Hardware Specifically for GNU/Linux

There are several vendors, who ship systems with Debian or other distributions of GNU/Linux *pre-installed*[6]. You might pay more for the privilege, but it does buy a level of peace of mind, since you can be sure that the hardware is well-supported by GNU/Linux.

---

[5] *http://www.tldp.org/HOWTO/Hardware-HOWTO.html*

Installation Guide

If you do have to buy a machine with Windows bundled, carefully read the software license that comes with Windows; you may be able to reject the license and obtain a rebate from your vendor. Searching the Internet for "windows refund" may get you some useful information to help with that.

Whether or not you are purchasing a system with Linux bundled, or even a used system, it is still important to check that your hardware is supported by the Linux kernel. Check if your hardware is listed in the references found above. Let your salesperson (if any) know that you're shopping for a Linux system. Support Linux-friendly hardware vendors.

2.3.1. Avoid Proprietary or Closed Hardware

Some hardware manufacturers simply won't tell us how to write drivers for their hardware. Others won't allow us access to the documentation without a non-disclosure agreement that would prevent us from releasing the Linux source code.

Since we haven't been granted access to the documentation on these devices, they simply won't work under Linux. You can help by asking the manufacturers of such hardware to release the documentation. If enough people ask, they will realize that the free software community is an important market.

2.3.2. Windows-specific Hardware

A disturbing trend is the proliferation of Windows-specific modems and printers. In some cases these are specially designed to be operated by the Microsoft Windows operating system and bear the legend "WinModem" or "Made especially for Windows-based computers". This is generally done by removing the embedded processors of the hardware and shifting the work they do over to a Windows driver that is run by your computer's main CPU. This strategy makes the hardware less expensive, but the savings are often *not* passed on to the user and this hardware may even be more expensive than equivalent devices that retain their embedded intelligence.

You should avoid Windows-specific hardware for two reasons. The first is that the manufacturers do not generally make the resources available to write a Linux driver. Generally, the hardware and software interface to the device is proprietary, and documentation is not available without a non-disclosure agreement, if it is available at all. This precludes it being used for free software, since free software writers disclose the source code of their programs. The second reason is that when devices like these have had their embedded processors removed, the operating system must perform the work of the embedded processors, often at *real-time* priority, and thus the CPU is not available to run

---

[6] *http://www.debian.org/distrib/pre-installed*

Ubuntu 9.10

your programs while it is driving these devices. Since the typical Windows user does not multi-process as intensively as a Linux user, the manufacturers hope that the Windows user simply won't notice the burden this hardware places on their CPU. However, any multi-processing operating system, even Windows 2000 or XP, suffers from degraded performance when peripheral manufacturers skimp on the embedded processing power of their hardware.

You can help improve this situation by encouraging these manufacturers to release the documentation and other resources necessary for us to program their hardware, but the best strategy is simply to avoid this sort of hardware until it is listed as working in the *Linux Hardware Compatibility HOWTO*[7].

2.4. Installation Media

This section will help you determine which different media types you can use to install Ubuntu. For example, if you have a floppy disk drive on your machine, it can be used to install Ubuntu. There is a whole chapter devoted to media, *Chapter 4, Obtaining System Installation Media*, which lists the advantages and disadvantages of each media type. You may want to refer back to this page once you reach that section.

2.4.1. CD-ROM/DVD-ROM

Note

Whenever you see "CD-ROM" in this manual, it applies to both CD-ROMs and DVD-ROMs, because both technologies are really the same from the operating system's point of view, except for some very old nonstandard CD-ROM drives which are neither SCSI nor IDE/ATAPI.

CD-ROM based installation is supported for some architectures. On machines which support bootable CD-ROMs, you should be able to do a completely floppy-less installation. Even if your system doesn't support booting from a CD-ROM, you can use the CD-ROM in conjunction with the other techniques to install your system, once you've booted up by other means; see *Chapter 5, Booting the Installation System*.

SCSI, SATA and IDE/ATAPI CD-ROMs are supported. The *Linux CD-ROM HOWTO*[8] contains in-depth information on using CD-ROMs with Linux.

USB CD-ROM drives are also supported, as are FireWire devices that are supported by the ohci1394 and sbp2 drivers.

---

[7] *http://www.tldp.org/HOWTO/Hardware-HOWTO.html*
[8] *http://www.tldp.org/HOWTO/CDROM-HOWTO.html*

Installation Guide

2.4.2. Hard Disk

Booting the installation system directly from a hard disk is another option for many architectures. This will require some other operating system to load the installer onto the hard disk.

2.4.3. USB Memory Stick

Many Ubuntu boxes need their floppy and/or CD-ROM drives only for setting up the system and for rescue purposes. If you operate some servers, you will probably already have thought about omitting those drives and using an USB memory stick for installing and (when necessary) for recovering the system. This is also useful for small systems which have no room for unnecessary drives.

2.4.4. Network

The network can be used during the installation to retrieve files needed for the installation. Whether the network is used or not depends on the installation method you choose and your answers to certain questions that will be asked during the installation. The installation system supports most types of network connections (including PPPoE, but not ISDN or PPP), via either HTTP or FTP. After the installation is completed, you can also configure your system to use ISDN and PPP.

You can also *boot* the installation system over the network.

Diskless installation, using network booting from a local area network and NFS-mounting of all local filesystems, is another option.

2.4.5. Un*x or GNU system

If you are running another Unix-like system, you could use it to install Ubuntu without using the `debian-installer` described in the rest of this manual. This kind of install may be useful for users with otherwise unsupported hardware or on hosts which can't afford downtime. If you are interested in this technique, skip to the *the section called "Installing Ubuntu from a Unix/Linux System"*.

2.4.6. Supported Storage Systems

The Ubuntu boot disks contain a kernel which is built to maximize the number of systems it runs on. Unfortunately, this makes for a larger kernel, which includes many drivers that won't be used for your machine (see *the section called "Compiling a New Kernel"* to learn how to build your own kernel). Support for the widest possible range of devices is desirable in general, to ensure that Ubuntu can be installed on the widest array of hardware.

Ubuntu 9.10

Generally, the Ubuntu installation system includes support for floppies, IDE (also known as PATA) drives, IDE floppies, parallel port IDE devices, SATA and SCSI controllers and drives, USB, and FireWire. The supported file systems include FAT, Win-32 FAT extensions (VFAT) and NTFS.

Disk interfaces that emulate the "AT" hard disk interface — often called MFM, RLL, IDE, or PATA — are supported. SATA and SCSI disk controllers from many different manufacturers are supported. See the *Linux Hardware Compatibility HOWTO*[9] for more details.

2.5. Memory and Disk Space Requirements

You must have at least 44MB of memory and 500MB of hard disk space to perform a normal installation. Note that these are fairly minimal numbers. For more realistic figures, see *the section called "Meeting Minimum Hardware Requirements"*.

Installation on systems with less memory[10] or disk space available may be possible but is only advised for experienced users.

---

[9] *http://www.tldp.org/HOWTO/Hardware-HOWTO.html*
[10] Installation images that support the graphical installer require more memory than images that support only the textual installer and should not be used on systems with less than 44MB of memory. If there is a choice between booting the regular and the graphical installer, the former should be selected.

Chapter 3.
Before Installing Ubuntu

This chapter deals with the preparation for installing Ubuntu before you even boot the installer. This includes backing up your data, gathering information about your hardware, and locating any necessary information.

3.1. Overview of the Installation Process

First, just a note about re-installations. With Ubuntu, a circumstance that will require a complete re-installation of your system is very rare; perhaps mechanical failure of the hard disk would be the most common case.

Many common operating systems may require a complete installation to be performed when critical failures take place or for upgrades to new OS versions. Even if a completely new installation isn't required, often the programs you use must be re-installed to operate properly in the new OS.

Under Ubuntu, it is much more likely that your OS can be repaired rather than replaced if things go wrong. Upgrades never require a wholesale installation; you can always upgrade in-place. And the programs are almost always compatible with successive OS releases. If a new program version requires newer supporting software, the Ubuntu packaging system ensures that all the necessary software is automatically identified and installed. The point is, much effort has been put into avoiding the need for re-installation, so think of it as your very last option. The installer is *not* designed to re-install over an existing system.

Here's a road map for the steps you will take during the installation process.

1. Back up any existing data or documents on the hard disk where you plan to install.
2. Gather information about your computer and any needed documentation, before starting the installation.
3. Create partitionable space for Ubuntu on your hard disk.
4. Locate and/or download the installer software and any specialized driver files your machine requires (except Ubuntu CD users).

5. Set up boot tapes/floppies/USB sticks, or place boot files (most Ubuntu CD users can boot from one of the CDs).
6. Boot the installation system.
7. Select the installation language.
8. Activate the ethernet network connection, if available.
9. Create and mount the partitions on which Ubuntu will be installed.
10. Watch the automatic download/install/setup of the *base system*.
11. Install a *boot loader* which can start up Ubuntu and/or your existing system.
12. Load the newly installed system for the first time.

For Intel x86 you have the option of using a graphical version of the installation system. For more information about this graphical installer, see *the section called "The Graphical Installer"*.

If you have problems during the installation, it helps to know which packages are involved in which steps. Introducing the leading software actors in this installation drama:

The installer software, `debian-installer`, is the primary concern of this manual. It detects hardware and loads appropriate drivers, uses `dhcp-client` to set up the network connection, runs `debootstrap` to install the base system packages, and runs `tasksel` to allow you to install certain additional software. Many more actors play smaller parts in this process, but `debian-installer` has completed its task when you load the new system for the first time.

To tune the system to your needs, `tasksel` allows you to choose to install various predefined bundles of software like a Web server or a Desktop environment.

Just be aware that the X Window System is completely separate from `debian-installer`, and in fact is much more complicated. Installation and troubleshooting of the X Window System is not within the scope of this manual.

3.2. Back Up Your Existing Data!

Before you start, make sure to back up every file that is now on your system. If this is the first time a non-native operating system has been installed on your computer, it's quite likely you will need to re-partition your disk to make room for Ubuntu. Anytime you partition your disk, you run a risk of losing everything on the disk, no matter what program you use to do it. The programs used in installation are quite reliable and most have seen years of use; but they are also quite powerful and a false move can cost you. Even after backing up, be careful and think about your answers and actions. Two minutes of thinking can save hours of unnecessary work.

If you are creating a multi-boot system, make sure that you have the distribution media of any other present operating systems on hand. Especially if you repartition your boot drive, you might find that you have to reinstall your operating system's boot loader, or in many cases the whole operating system itself and all files on the affected partitions.

3.3. Information You Will Need

3.3.1. Documentation

3.3.1.1. Installation Manual

The document you are now reading, which is the official version of the Installation Guide for the jaunty release of Ubuntu.

3.3.1.2. Hardware documentation

Often contains useful information on configuring or using your hardware.

- *Linux Hardware Compatibility HOWTO*[1]

3.3.2. Finding Sources of Hardware Information

In many cases, the installer will be able to automatically detect your hardware. But to be prepared, we do recommend familiarizing yourself with your hardware before the install.

Hardware information can be gathered from:

- The manuals that come with each piece of hardware.
- The BIOS setup screens of your computer. You can view these screens when you start your computer by pressing a combination of keys. Check your manual for the combination. Often, it is the **Delete** key.
- The cases and boxes for each piece of hardware.
- The System window in the Windows Control Panel.
- System commands or tools in another operating system, including file manager displays. This source is especially useful for information about RAM and hard drive memory.
- Your system administrator or Internet Service Provider. These sources can tell you the settings you need to set up your networking and e-mail.

---

[1] *http://www.tldp.org/HOWTO/Hardware-HOWTO.html*

Ubuntu 9.10

Hardware	Information You Might Need
Hard Drives	How many you have.
	Their order on the system.
	Whether IDE (also known as PATA), SATA or SCSI.
	Available free space.
	Partitions.
	Partitions where other operating systems are installed.
Monitor	Model and manufacturer.
	Resolutions supported.
	Horizontal refresh rate.
	Vertical refresh rate.
	Color depth (number of colors) supported.
	Screen size.
Mouse	Type: serial, PS/2, or USB.
	Port.
	Manufacturer.
	Number of buttons.
Network	Model and manufacturer.
	Type of adapter.
Printer	Model and manufacturer.
	Printing resolutions supported.
Video Card	Model and manufacturer.
	Video RAM available.
	Resolutions and color depths supported (these should be checked against your monitor's capabilities).

Table 3.1. Hardware Information Needed for an Install

3.3.3. Hardware Compatibility

Many brand name products work without trouble on Linux. Moreover, hardware support in Linux is improving daily. However, Linux still does not run as many different types of hardware as some operating systems.

In particular, Linux usually cannot run hardware that requires a running version of Windows to work.

Although some Windows-specific hardware can be made to run on Linux, doing so usually requires extra effort. In addition, Linux drivers for Windows-specific hardware are usually specific to one Linux kernel. Therefore, they can quickly become obsolete.

So called win-modems are the most common type of this hardware. However, printers and other equipment may also be Windows-specific.

You can check hardware compatibility by:

- Checking manufacturers' web sites for new drivers.
- Looking at web sites or manuals for information about emulation. Lesser known brands can sometimes use the drivers or settings for better-known ones.
- Checking hardware compatibility lists for Linux on web sites dedicated to your architecture.
- Searching the Internet for other users' experiences.

3.3.4. Network Settings

If your computer is connected to a network 24 hours a day (i.e., an Ethernet or equivalent connection — not a PPP connection), you should ask your network's system administrator for this information.

- Your host name (you may be able to decide this on your own).
- Your domain name.
- Your computer's IP address.
- The netmask to use with your network.
- The IP address of the default gateway system you should route to, if your network *has* a gateway.
- The system on your network that you should use as a DNS (Domain Name Service) server.

On the other hand, if your administrator tells you that a DHCP server is available and is recommended, then you don't need this information because the DHCP server will provide it directly to your computer during the installation process.

If you use a wireless network, you should also find out:

- ESSID of your wireless network.
- WEP security key (if applicable).

3.4. Meeting Minimum Hardware Requirements

Once you have gathered information about your computer's hardware, check that your hardware will let you do the type of installation that you want to do.

Depending on your needs, you might manage with less than some of the recommended hardware listed in the table below. However, most users risk being frustrated if they ignore these suggestions.

A Pentium 4, 1GHz system is the minimum recommended for a desktop system.

Install Type	RAM (minimal)	RAM (recommended)	Hard Drive
No desktop	64 megabytes	256 megabytes	1 gigabyte
With Desktop	64 megabytes	512 megabytes	5 gigabytes

Table 3.2. Recommended Minimum System Requirements

The actual minimum memory requirements are a lot less then the numbers listed in this table. Depending on the architecture, it is possible to install Ubuntu with as little as 20MB (for s390) to 48MB (for i386 and amd64). The same goes for the disk space requirements, especially if you pick and choose which applications to install; see *the section called "Disk Space Needed"* for additional information on disk space requirements.

It is possible to run a graphical desktop environment on older or low-end systems, but in that case it is recommended to install a window manager that is less resource-hungry than those of the GNOME or KDE desktop environments; alternatives include `xfce4`, `icewm` and `wmaker`, but there are others to choose from.

It is practically impossible to give general memory or disk space requirements for server installations as those very much depend on what the server is to be used for.

Remember that these sizes don't include all the other materials which are usually to be found, such as user files, mail, and data. It is always best to be generous when considering the space for your own files and data.

Disk space required for the smooth operation of the Debian GNU/Linux system itself is taken into account in these recommended system requirements. Notably, the `/var` partition contains a lot of state information specific to Ubuntu in addition to its regular contents, like logfiles. The **dpkg** files (with information on all installed packages) can easily consume 40MB. Also, **apt-get** puts downloaded packages here before they are installed. You should usually allocate at least 200MB for `/var`, and a lot more if you install a graphical desktop environment.

Installation Guide

3.5. Pre-Partitioning for Multi-Boot Systems

Partitioning your disk simply refers to the act of breaking up your disk into sections. Each section is then independent of the others. It's roughly equivalent to putting up walls inside a house; if you add furniture to one room it doesn't affect any other room.

If you already have an operating system on your system (Windows 9x, Windows NT/2000/XP, OS/2, MacOS, Solaris, FreeBSD, ...) and want to stick Linux on the same disk, you will need to repartition the disk. Ubuntu requires its own hard disk partitions. It cannot be installed on Windows or MacOS partitions. It may be able to share some partitions with other Linux systems, but that's not covered here. At the very least you will need a dedicated partition for the Ubuntu root.

You can find information about your current partition setup by using a partitioning tool for your current operating system , such as fdisk or PartitionMagic. Partitioning tools always provide a way to show existing partitions without making changes.

In general, changing a partition with a file system already on it will destroy any information there. Thus you should always make backups before doing any repartitioning. Using the analogy of the house, you would probably want to move all the furniture out of the way before moving a wall or you risk destroying it.

If your computer has more than one hard disk, you may want to dedicate one of the hard disks completely to Ubuntu. If so, you don't need to partition that disk before booting the installation system; the installer's included partitioning program can handle the job nicely.

If your machine has only one hard disk, and you would like to completely replace the current operating system with Ubuntu, you also can wait to partition as part of the installation process (*the section called "Partitioning and Mount Point Selection"*), after you have booted the installation system. However this only works if you plan to boot the installer system from tapes, CD-ROM or files on a connected machine. Consider: if you boot from files placed on the hard disk, and then partition that same hard disk within the installation system, thus erasing the boot files, you'd better hope the installation is successful the first time around. At the least in this case, you should have some alternate means of reviving your machine like the original system's installation tapes or CDs.

If your machine already has multiple partitions, and enough space can be provided by deleting and replacing one or more of them, then you too can wait and use the Ubuntu installer's partitioning program. You should still read through the material below, because there may be special circumstances like the order of the existing partitions within the partition map, that force you to partition before installing anyway.

If your machine has a FAT or NTFS filesystem, as used by DOS and Windows, you can wait and use Ubuntu installer's partitioning program to resize the filesystem.

Ubuntu 9.10

If none of the above apply, you'll need to partition your hard disk before starting the installation to create partitionable space for Ubuntu. If some of the partitions will be owned by other operating systems, you should create those partitions using native operating system partitioning programs. We recommend that you do *not* attempt to create partitions for Ubuntu using another operating system's tools. Instead, you should just create the native operating system's partitions you will want to retain.

If you are going to install more than one operating system on the same machine, you should install all other system(s) before proceeding with Linux installation. Windows and other OS installations may destroy your ability to start Linux, or encourage you to reformat non-native partitions.

You can recover from these actions or avoid them, but installing the native system first saves you trouble.

If you currently have one hard disk with one partition (a common setup for desktop computers), and you want to multi-boot the native operating system and Ubuntu, you will need to:

1. Back up everything on the computer.
2. Boot from the native operating system installer media such as CD-ROM or tapes.
3. Use the native partitioning tools to create native system partition(s). Leave either a place holder partition or free space for Ubuntu.
4. Install the native operating system on its new partition.
5. Boot back into the native system to verify everything's OK, and to download the Ubuntu installer boot files.
6. Boot the Ubuntu installer to continue installing Ubuntu.

3.5.1. Partitioning From DOS or Windows

If you are manipulating existing FAT or NTFS partitions, it is recommended that you either use the scheme below or native Windows or DOS tools. Otherwise, it is not really necessary to partition from DOS or Windows; the Linux partitioning tools will generally do a better job.

But if you have a large IDE disk, and are not using LBA addressing, overlay drivers (sometimes provided by hard disk manufacturers), or a new (post 1998) BIOS that supports large disk access extensions, then you must locate your Ubuntu boot partition carefully. In this case, you will have to put the boot partition into the first 1024 cylinders of your hard disk (usually around 524 megabytes, without BIOS translation). This may require that you move an existing FAT or NTFS partition.

Installation Guide

3.5.1.1. Lossless Repartitioning When Starting From DOS, Win-32 or OS/2

One of the most common installations is onto a system that already contains DOS (including Windows 3.1), Win32 (such as Windows 95, 98, Me, NT, 2000, XP), or OS/2, and it is desired to put Ubuntu onto the same disk without destroying the previous system. Note that the installer supports resizing of FAT and NTFS filesystems as used by DOS and Windows. Simply start the installer and when you get to the partitioning step, select the option for Manual partitioning, select the partition to resize, and specify its new size. So in most cases you should not need to use the method described below.

Before going any further, you should have decided how you will be dividing up the disk. The method in this section will only split a partition into two pieces. One will contain the original OS and the other will be used for Ubuntu. During the installation of Ubuntu, you will be given the opportunity to use the Ubuntu portion of the disk as you see fit, i.e., as swap or as a file system.

The idea is to move all the data on the partition to the beginning, before changing the partition information, so that nothing will be lost. It is important that you do as little as possible between the data movement and repartitioning to minimize the chance of a file being written near the end of the partition as this will decrease the amount of space you can take from the partition.

The first thing needed is a copy of **fips** which is available in the `tools/` directory on your nearest Ubuntu mirror. Unzip the archive and copy the files `RESTORRB.EXE`, `FIPS.EXE` and `ERRORS.TXT` to a bootable floppy. A bootable floppy can be created using the command `sys a:` under DOS. **fips** comes with very good documentation which you may want to read. You will definitely need to read the documentation if you use a disk compression driver or a disk manager. Create the disk and read the documentation *before* you defragment the disk.

The next thing needed is to move all the data to the beginning of the partition. **defrag**, which comes standard with DOS 6.0 and later, can easily do the job. See the **fips** documentation for a list of other software that may do the trick. Note that if you have Windows 9x, you must run **defrag** from there, since DOS doesn't understand VFAT, which is used to support for long filenames, used in Windows 95 and higher.

After running the defragmenter (which can take a while on a large disk), reboot with the **fips** disk you created in the floppy drive. Simply type `a:\fips` and follow the directions.

Note that there are many other partition managers out there, in case **fips** doesn't do the trick for you.

3.5.1.2. Partitioning for DOS

If you are partitioning for DOS drives, or changing the size of DOS partitions, using Linux tools, many people experience problems working with the resulting FAT partitions. For

39

instance, some have reported slow performance, consistent problems with **scandisk**, or other weird errors in DOS or Windows.

Apparently, whenever you create or resize a partition for DOS use, it's a good idea to fill the first few sectors with zeros. You should do this prior to running DOS's **format** command by executing the following command from Linux:

```
# dd if=/dev/zero of=/dev/hdXX bs=512 count=4
```

3.6. Pre-Installation Hardware and Operating System Setup

This section will walk you through pre-installation hardware setup, if any, that you will need to do prior to installing Ubuntu. Generally, this involves checking and possibly changing firmware settings for your system. The "firmware" is the core software used by the hardware; it is most critically invoked during the bootstrap process (after power-up). Known hardware issues affecting the reliability of Ubuntu on your system are also highlighted.

3.6.1. Invoking the BIOS Set-Up Menu

BIOS provides the basic functions needed to boot your machine to allow your operating system to access your hardware. Your system probably provides a BIOS setup menu, which is used to configure the BIOS. Before installing, you *must* ensure that your BIOS is set up correctly; not doing so can lead to intermittent crashes or an inability to install Ubuntu.

The rest of this section is lifted from the *http://www.faqs.org/faqs/pc-hardware-faq/part1/*, answering the question, "How do I enter the CMOS configuration menu?". How you access the BIOS (or "CMOS") configuration menu depends on who wrote your BIOS software:

AMI BIOS

    Delete key during the POST (power on self test)

Award BIOS

    Ctrl+ Alt+ Esc, or **Delete** key during the POST

DTK BIOS

    Esc key during the POST

IBM PS/2 BIOS

    Ctrl+ Alt+ Insert after **Ctrl+ Alt+ Delete**

Phoenix BIOS

    Ctrl+ Alt+ Esc or **Ctrl+ Alt+ S** or **F1**

Installation Guide

Information on invoking other BIOS routines can be found in
http://www.tldp.org/HOWTO/Hard-Disk-Upgrade/install.html.

Some Intel x86 machines don't have a CMOS configuration menu in the BIOS. They require a software CMOS setup program. If you don't have the Installation and/or Diagnostics diskette for your machine, you can try using a shareware/freeware program. Try looking in *ftp://ftp.simtel.net/pub/simtelnet/msdos/*.

3.6.2. Boot Device Selection

Many BIOS setup menus allow you to select the devices that will be used to bootstrap the system. Set this to look for a bootable operating system on A: (the first floppy disk), then optionally the first CD-ROM device (possibly appearing as D: or E:), and then from C: (the first hard disk). This setting enables you to boot from either a floppy disk or a CD-ROM, which are the two most common boot devices used to install Ubuntu.

If you have a newer SCSI controller and you have a CD-ROM device attached to it, you are usually able to boot from the CD-ROM. All you have to do is enable booting from a CD-ROM in the SCSI-BIOS of your controller.

Another popular option is to boot from a USB storage device (also called a USB memory stick or USB key). Some BIOSes can boot directly from a USB storage device, but some cannot. You may need to configure your BIOS to boot from a "Removable drive" or even from "USB-ZIP" to get it to boot from the USB device.

Here are some details about how to set the boot order. Remember to reset the boot order after Linux is installed, so that you restart your machine from the hard drive.

3.6.2.1. Changing the Boot Order on IDE Computers

1. As your computer starts, press the keys to enter the BIOS utility. Often, it is the **Delete** key. However, consult the hardware documentation for the exact keystrokes.
2. Find the boot sequence in the setup utility. Its location depends on your BIOS, but you are looking for a field that lists drives.
3. Common entries on IDE machines are C, A, cdrom or A, C, cdrom.
4. C is the hard drive, and A is the floppy drive.
5. Change the boot sequence setting so that the CD-ROM or the floppy is first. Usually, the **Page Up** or **Page Down** keys cycle through the possible choices.
6. Save your changes. Instructions on the screen tell you how to save the changes on your computer.

Ubuntu 9.10

3.6.2.2. Changing the Boot Order on SCSI Computers

1. As your computer starts, press the keys to enter the SCSI setup utility.

    You can start the SCSI setup utility after the memory check and the message about how to start the BIOS utility displays when you start your computer.

    The keystrokes you need depend on the utility. Often, it is **Ctrl+ F2**. However, consult your hardware documentation for the exact keystrokes.

2. Find the utility for changing the boot order.
3. Set the utility so that the SCSI ID of the CD drive is first on the list.
4. Save your changes. Instructions on the screen tell you how to save the changes on your computer. Often, you must press **F10**.

3.6.3. Miscellaneous BIOS Settings

3.6.3.1. CD-ROM Settings

Some BIOS systems (such as Award BIOS) allow you to automatically set the CD speed. You should avoid that, and instead set it to, say, the lowest speed. If you get `seek failed` error messages, this may be your problem.

3.6.3.2. Extended vs. Expanded Memory

If your system provides both ex *ten*ded and ex *pan*ded memory, set it so that there is as much extended and as little expanded memory as possible. Linux requires extended memory and cannot use expanded memory.

3.6.3.3. Virus Protection

Disable any virus-warning features your BIOS may provide. If you have a virus-protection board or other special hardware, make sure it is disabled or physically removed while running GNU/Linux. These aren't compatible with GNU/Linux; moreover, due to the file system permissions and protected memory of the Linux kernel, viruses are almost unheard of[2].

3.6.3.4. Shadow RAM

Your motherboard may provide *shadow RAM* or BIOS caching. You may see settings for "Video BIOS Shadow", "C800-CBFF Shadow", etc. *Disable* all shadow RAM. Shadow RAM is

---

[2] After installation you can enable Boot Sector protection if you want. This offers no additional security in Linux but if you also run Windows it may prevent a catastrophe. There is no need to tamper with the Master Boot Record (MBR) after the boot manager has been set up.

used to accelerate access to the ROMs on your motherboard and on some of the controller cards. Linux does not use these ROMs once it has booted because it provides its own faster 32-bit software in place of the 16-bit programs in the ROMs. Disabling the shadow RAM may make some of it available for programs to use as normal memory. Leaving the shadow RAM enabled may interfere with Linux access to hardware devices.

3.6.3.5. Memory Hole

If your BIOS offers something like "15–16 MB Memory Hole", please disable that. Linux expects to find memory there if you have that much RAM.

We have a report of an Intel Endeavor motherboard on which there is an option called "LFB" or "Linear Frame Buffer". This had two settings: "Disabled" and "1 Megabyte". Set it to "1 Megabyte". When disabled, the installation floppy was not read correctly, and the system eventually crashed. At this writing we don't understand what's going on with this particular device — it just worked with that setting and not without it.

3.6.3.6. Advanced Power Management

If your motherboard provides Advanced Power Management (APM), configure it so that power management is controlled by APM. Disable the doze, standby, suspend, nap, and sleep modes, and disable the hard disk's power-down timer. Linux can take over control of these modes, and can do a better job of power-management than the BIOS.

3.6.4. Hardware Issues to Watch Out For

USB BIOS support and keyboards. If you have no AT-style keyboard and only a USB model, you may need to enable legacy AT keyboard emulation in your BIOS setup. Only do this if the installation system fails to use your keyboard in USB mode. Conversely, for some systems (especially laptops) you may need to disable legacy USB support if your keyboard does not respond. Consult your main board manual and look in the BIOS for "Legacy keyboard emulation" or "USB keyboard support" options.

Chapter 4.
Obtaining System Installation Media

4.1. Official Ubuntu CD-ROMs

By far the easiest way to install Ubuntu is from an *Official Ubuntu CD-ROM*[1]. You may download the CD-ROM image from an Ubuntu mirror and make your own CD, if you have a fast network connection and a CD burner. If you have an Ubuntu CD and CDs are bootable on your machine, you can skip right to *Chapter 5, Booting the Installation System*; much effort has been expended to ensure the files most people need are there on the CD.

If your machine doesn't support CD booting, but you do have a CD, you can use an alternative strategy such as hard disk, usb stick, net boot, or manually loading the kernel from the CD to initially boot the system installer. The files you need for booting by another means are also on the CD; the Ubuntu network archive and CD folder organization are identical. So when archive file paths are given below for particular files you need for booting, look for those files in the same directories and subdirectories on your CD.

Once the installer is booted, it will be able to obtain all the other files it needs from the CD.

If you don't have a CD, then you will need to download the installer system files and place them on the hard disk or usb stick or a connected computer so they can be used to boot the installer.

4.2. Downloading Files from Ubuntu Mirrors

To find the nearest (and thus probably the fastest) mirror, see the *list of Ubuntu mirrors*[2].

When downloading files from an Ubuntu mirror using FTP, be sure to download the files in *binary* mode, not text or automatic mode.

---

[1] *http://releases.ubuntu.com/jaunty/*
[2] *http://wiki.ubuntu.com/Archive*

Installation Guide

4.2.1. Where to Find Installation Images

The installation images are located on each Ubuntu mirror in the directory *ubuntu/dists/jaunty/main/installer-i386/current/images/*[3] — the *MANIFEST*[4] lists each image and its purpose.

4.3. Preparing Files for USB Memory Stick Booting

There are two installation methods possible when booting from USB stick. The first is to install completely from the network. The second is to also copy a CD image onto the USB stick and use that as a source for packages, possibly in combination with a mirror. This second method is the more common.

For the first installation method you'll need to download an installer image from the `netboot` directory (at the location mentioned in *the section called "Where to Find Installation Images"*) and use the "flexible way" explained below to copy the files to the USB stick.

Installation images for the second installation method can be found in the `hd-media` directory and either the "easy way" or the "flexible way" can be used to copy the image to the USB stick. For this installation method you will also need to download a CD image. The installation image and the CD image must be based on the same release of `debian-installer`. If they do not match you are likely to get errors[5] during the installation.

To prepare the USB stick, you will need a system where GNU/Linux is already running and where USB is supported. With current GNU/Linux systems the USB stick should be automatically recognized when you insert it. If it is not you should check that the usb-storage kernel module is loaded. When the USB stick is inserted, it will be mapped to a device named `/dev/sdX`, where the "X" is a letter in the range a-z. You should be able to see to which device the USB stick was mapped by running the command **dmesg** after inserting it. To write to your stick, you may have to turn off its write protection switch.

> ⚠ **Warning**
>
> The procedures described in this section will destroy anything already on the device! Make very sure that you use the correct device name for your USB stick. If you use the wrong device the result could be that all information on for example a hard disk could be lost.

---

[3] *http://archive.ubuntu.com/ubuntu/dists/jaunty/main/installer-i386/current/images*
[4] *http://archive.ubuntu.com/ubuntu/dists/jaunty/main/installer-i386/current/images/MANIFEST*
[5] The error message that is most likely to be displayed is that no kernel modules can be found. This means that the version of the kernel module udebs included on the CD image is different from the version of the running kernel.

Ubuntu 9.10

Note that the USB stick should be at least 8 MB in size. If you follow *the section called "Copying the files — the flexible way"* and want to include an Ubuntu ISO image on the stick, you will need enough space for the ISO as well.

4.3.1. Copying the files — the easy way

There is an all-in-one file *netboot/boot.img.gz*[6] which contains all the installer files (including the kernel) as well as `syslinux` and its configuration file.

To use this image you only have to extract it directly to a partition on your USB stick:

```
# zcat boot.img.gz > /dev/sdX1
```

4.3.2. Copying the files — the flexible way

If you like more flexibility or just want to know what's going on, you should use the following method to put the files on your stick. One advantage of using this method is that — if the capacity of your USB stick is large enough — you have the option of copying a full CD ISO image to it.

4.3.2.1. Partitioning the USB stick

We will show how to set up the memory stick to use the first partition, instead of the entire device.

> **Note**
>
> Since most USB sticks come pre-configured with a single FAT16 partition, you probably won't have to repartition or reformat the stick. If you have to do that anyway, use **cfdisk** or any other partitioning tool to create a FAT16 partition, and then create the filesystem using:
>
> ```
> # mkdosfs /dev/sdX1
> ```
>
> Take care that you use the correct device name for your USB stick. The **mkdosfs** command is contained in the `dosfstools` Ubuntu package.

In order to start the kernel after booting from the USB stick, we will put a boot loader on the stick. Although any boot loader (e.g. `lilo`) should work, it's convenient to use `syslinux`, since it uses a FAT16 partition and can be reconfigured by just editing a text file. Any operating system which supports the FAT file system can be used to make changes to the configuration of the boot loader.

To put `syslinux` on the FAT16 partition on your USB stick, install the `syslinux` and `mtools` packages on your system, and do:

---

[6] http://archive.ubuntu.com/ubuntu/dists/jaunty/main/installer-i386/current/images/netboot/boot.img.gz

```
# syslinux /dev/sdX1
```

Again, take care that you use the correct device name. The partition must not be mounted when starting **syslinux**. This procedure writes a boot sector to the partition and creates the file `ldlinux.sys` which contains the boot loader code.

4.3.2.2. Adding the installer image

Mount the partition (`mount /dev/ sdX1 /mnt`) and copy the following installer image files to the stick:

- `vmlinuz` (kernel binary)
- `initrd.gz` (initial ramdisk image)

You can choose between either the regular version or the graphical version of the installer. The latter can be found in the `gtk` subdirectory. If you want to rename the files, please note that `syslinux` can only process DOS (8.3) file names.

Next you should create a `syslinux.cfg` configuration file, which at a bare minimum should contain the following two lines:

```
default vmlinuz
append initrd=initrd.gz
```

For the graphical installer you should add `video=vesa:ywrap,mtrr vga=788` to the second line.

If you used an `hd-media` image, you should now copy an Ubuntu ISO image (businesscard, netinst or full CD image; be sure to select one that fits) onto the stick. When you are done, unmount the USB memory stick (`umount /mnt`).

4.3.3. Booting the USB stick

> **Warning**
>
> If your system refuses to boot from the memory stick, the stick may contain an invalid master boot record (MBR). To fix this, use the **install-mbr** command from the package mbr:
> ```
> # install-mbr /dev/sdX
> ```

4.4. Preparing Files for Hard Disk Booting

The installer may be booted using boot files placed on an existing hard drive partition, either launched from another operating system or by invoking a boot loader directly from the BIOS.

A full, "pure network" installation can be achieved using this technique. This avoids all hassles of removable media, like finding and burning CD images or struggling with too numerous and unreliable floppy disks.

The installer cannot boot from files on an NTFS file system.

4.4.1. Hard disk installer booting using LILO or GRUB

This section explains how to add to or even replace an existing linux installation using either **LILO** or **GRUB**.

At boot time, both bootloaders support loading in memory not only the kernel, but also a disk image. This RAM disk can be used as the root file-system by the kernel.

Copy the following files from the Ubuntu archives to a convenient location on your hard drive, for instance to `/boot/newinstall/`.

- `vmlinuz` (kernel binary)
- `initrd.gz` (ramdisk image)

Finally, to configure the bootloader proceed to *the section called "Booting from Linux Using LILO or GRUB"*.

4.5. Preparing Files for TFTP Net Booting

If your machine is connected to a local area network, you may be able to boot it over the network from another machine, using TFTP. If you intend to boot the installation system from another machine, the boot files will need to be placed in specific locations on that machine, and the machine configured to support booting of your specific machine.

You need to set up a TFTP server, and for many machines a DHCP server , or BOOTP server.

BOOTP is an IP protocol that informs a computer of its IP address and where on the network to obtain a boot image. The DHCP (Dynamic Host Configuration Protocol) is a more flexible, backwards-compatible extension of BOOTP. Some systems can only be configured via DHCP.

The Trivial File Transfer Protocol (TFTP) is used to serve the boot image to the client. Theoretically, any server, on any platform, which implements these protocols, may be used. In the examples in this section, we shall provide commands for SunOS 4.x, SunOS 5.x (a.k.a. Solaris), and GNU/Linux.

> **Note**
>
> To use the Pre-boot Execution Environment (PXE) method of TFTP booting, you will need a TFTP server with **tsize** support. On an Ubuntu or Debian GNU/Linux server, the `atftpd` and `tftpd-hpa` packages qualify; we recommend `tftpd-hpa`.

Installation Guide

4.5.1. Setting up a BOOTP server

There are two BOOTP servers available for GNU/Linux. The first is CMU **bootpd**. The other is actually a DHCP server: ISC **dhcpd**. In Ubuntu these are contained in the `bootp` and `dhcp3-server` packages respectively.

To use CMU **bootpd**, you must first uncomment (or add) the relevant line in `/etc/inetd.conf`. On Debian GNU/Linux or Ubuntu, you can run **update-inetd -- enable bootps**, then **/etc/init.d/inetd reload** to do so. Just in case your BOOTP server does not run Debian or Ubuntu, the line in question should look like:

```
bootps  dgram  udp  wait  root  /usr/sbin/bootpd  bootpd -i -t 120
```

Now, you must create an `/etc/bootptab` file. This has the same sort of familiar and cryptic format as the good old BSD `printcap`, `termcap`, and `disktab` files. See the `bootptab` manual page for more information. For CMU **bootpd**, you will need to know the hardware (MAC) address of the client. Here is an example `/etc/bootptab`:

```
client:\
  hd=/tftpboot:\
  bf=tftpboot.img:\
  ip=192.168.1.90:\
  sm=255.255.255.0:\
  sa=192.168.1.1:\
  ha=0123456789AB:
```

You will need to change at least the "ha" option, which specifies the hardware address of the client. The "bf" option specifies the file a client should retrieve via TFTP; see *the section called "Move TFTP Images Into Place"* for more details.

By contrast, setting up BOOTP with ISC **dhcpd** is really easy, because it treats BOOTP clients as a moderately special case of DHCP clients. Some architectures require a complex configuration for booting clients via BOOTP. If yours is one of those, read the section *the section called "Setting up a DHCP server"*. In that case, you will probably be able to get away with simply adding the **allow bootp** directive to the configuration block for the subnet containing the client, and restart **dhcpd** with **/etc/init.d/dhcpd3-server restart**.

4.5.2. Setting up a DHCP server

One free software DHCP server is ISC **dhcpd**. For Ubuntu, the `dhcp3-server` package is recommended. Here is a sample configuration file for it (see `/etc/dhcp3/dhcpd.conf`):

```
option domain-name "example.com";
option domain-name-servers ns1.example.com;
option subnet-mask 255.255.255.0;
default-lease-time 600;
max-lease-time 7200;
server-name "servername";
```

49

Ubuntu 9.10

```
subnet 192.168.1.0 netmask 255.255.255.0 {
  range 192.168.1.200 192.168.1.253;
  option routers 192.168.1.1;
}

host clientname {
  filename "/tftpboot/tftpboot.img";
  server-name "servername";
  next-server servername;
  hardware ethernet 01:23:45:67:89:AB;
  fixed-address 192.168.1.90;
}
```

In this example, there is one server `servername` which performs all of the work of DHCP server, TFTP server, and network gateway. You will almost certainly need to change the domain-name options, as well as the server name and client hardware address. The `filename` option should be the name of the file which will be retrieved via TFTP.

After you have edited the **dhcpd** configuration file, restart it with **/etc/init.d/dhcpd3-server restart**.

4.5.2.1. Enabling PXE Booting in the DHCP configuration

Here is another example for a `dhcp.conf` using the Pre-boot Execution Environment (PXE) method of TFTP.

```
option domain-name "example.com";

default-lease-time 600;
max-lease-time 7200;

allow booting;
allow bootp;

# The next paragraph needs to be modified to fit your case
subnet 192.168.1.0 netmask 255.255.255.0 {
  range 192.168.1.200 192.168.1.253;
  option broadcast-address 192.168.1.255;
# the gateway address which can be different
# (access to the internet for instance)
  option routers 192.168.1.1;
# indicate the dns you want to use
  option domain-name-servers 192.168.1.3;
}

group {
  next-server 192.168.1.3;
  host tftpclient {
# tftp client hardware address
  hardware ethernet   00:10:DC:27:6C:15;
  filename "pxelinux.0";
 }
}
```

Note that for PXE booting, the client filename `pxelinux.0` is a boot loader, not a kernel image (see *the section called "Move TFTP Images Into Place"* below).

4.5.3. Enabling the TFTP Server

To get the TFTP server ready to go, you should first make sure that **tftpd** is enabled. This is usually enabled by having something like the following line in `/etc/inetd.conf`:

```
tftp dgram udp wait nobody /usr/sbin/tcpd in.tftpd /tftpboot
```

Ubuntu packages will in general set this up correctly by default when they are installed.

> **Note**
>
> Historically, TFTP servers used `/tftpboot` as directory to serve images from. However, Debian GNU/Linux packages may use other directories to comply with the *Filesystem Hierarchy Standard*[7]. For example, `tftpd-hpa` by default uses `/var/lib/tftpboot`. You may have to adjust the configuration examples in this section accordingly.

Look in `/etc/inetd.conf` and remember the directory which is used as the argument of **in.tftpd**[8]; you'll need that below. If you've had to change `/etc/inetd.conf`, you'll have to notify the running **inetd** process that the file has changed. On an Ubuntu or Debian machine, run `/etc/init.d/inetd reload`; on other machines, find out the process ID for **inetd**, and run `kill -HUP inetd-pid`.

4.5.4. Move TFTP Images Into Place

Next, place the TFTP boot image you need, as found in *the section called "Where to Find Installation Images"*, in the **tftpd** boot image directory. You may have to make a link from that file to the file which **tftpd** will use for booting a particular client. Unfortunately, the file name is determined by the TFTP client, and there are no strong standards.

For PXE booting, everything you should need is set up in the `netboot/netboot.tar.gz` tarball. Simply extract this tarball into the **tftpd** boot image directory. Make sure your dhcp server is configured to pass `pxelinux.0` to **tftpd** as the filename to boot.

4.6. Automatic Installation

For installing on multiple computers it's possible to do fully automatic installations. Ubuntu packages intended for this include `fai` (which uses an install server), `replicator`, `systemimager`, `autoinstall`, and the Ubuntu Installer itself.

---

[7] http://www.pathname.com/fhs/
[8] All **in.tftpd** alternatives available in Debian should log TFTP requests to the system logs by default. Some of them support a `-v` argument to increase verbosity. It is recommended to check these log messages in case of boot problems as they are a good starting point for diagnosing the cause of errors.

4.6.1. Automatic Installation Using the Ubuntu Installer

The Ubuntu Installer supports automating installs via preconfiguration files. A preconfiguration file can be loaded from the network or from removable media, and used to fill in answers to questions asked during the installation process.

Full documentation on preseeding including a working example that you can edit is in *Appendix B, Automating the installation using preseeding*.

4.6.2. Automatic Installation Using Kickstart

The Ubuntu installer has preliminary support for automating installs using Kickstart files, as designed by Red Hat for use in their Anaconda installer. This method is not as flexible as the preconfiguration file method above, but it requires less knowledge of how the installer works.

This section documents only the basics, and differences between Anaconda and the Ubuntu installer. Refer to the *Red Hat documentation*[9] for detailed instructions.

To generate a Kickstart file, install the system-config-kickstart package and run system-config-kickstart. This offers you a graphical user interface to the various options available.

Once you have a Kickstart file, you can edit it if necessary, and place it on a web, FTP, or NFS server, or copy it onto the installer's boot media. Wherever you place the file, you need to pass a parameter to the installer at boot time to tell it to use the file.

To make the installer use a Kickstart file downloaded from a web or FTP server, add ks=http://url/to/ks.cfg or ks=ftp://url/to/ks.cfg respectively to the kernel boot parameters. This requires the installer to be able to set up the network via DHCP on the first connected interface without asking any questions; you may also need to add ksdevice=eth1 or similar if the installer fails to determine the correct interface automatically.

Similarly, to make the installer use a Kickstart file on an NFS server, add ks=nfs:server:/path/to/ks.cfg to the kernel boot parameters. The method supported by Anaconda of adding a plain "ks" boot parameter to work out the location of the Kickstart file from a DHCP response is not yet supported by the Ubuntu installer.

To place a Kickstart file on a CD, you would need to remaster the ISO image to include your Kickstart file, and add ks=cdrom:/path/to/ks.cfg to the kernel boot parameters. See the manual page for mkisofs for details. Alternatively, put the Kickstart file on a floppy, and add ks=floppy:/path/to/ks.cfg to the kernel boot parameters.

---

[9] *http://www.redhat.com/docs/manuals/linux/RHL-9-Manual/custom-guide/part-install-info.html*

Installation Guide

4.6.2.1. Additions

The Ubuntu installer supports a few extensions to Kickstart that were needed to support automatic installations of Ubuntu:

- The `rootpw` command now takes the `--disabled` option to disable the root password. If this is used, the initial user will be given root privileges via sudo.
- A new `user` command has been added to control the creation of the initial user:
  ```
  user joe --fullname "Joe User" --password iamjoe
  ```
  The `--disabled` option prevents any non-root users from being created. The `--fullname` option specifies the user's full name, as opposed to the Unix username. The `--password` option supplies the user's password, by default in the clear (in which case make sure your Kickstart file is kept confidential!); the `--iscrypted` option may be used to state that the password is already MD5-hashed.
- A new `preseed` command has been added to provide a convenient way to preseed additional items in the debconf database that are not directly accessible using the ordinary Kickstart syntax:
  ```
  preseed --owner gdm shared/default-x-display-manager select gdm
  ```
  Note that if the value contains any special characters, then the value must be quoted, as follows:
  ```
  preseed preseed/late_command string "sed -i 's/foo/bar/g' /target/etc/hosts"
  ```
  The `--owner` option sets the name of the package that owns the question; if omitted, it defaults to d-i, which is generally appropriate for items affecting the first stage of the installer. The three mandatory arguments are the question name, question type, and answer, in that order, just as would be supplied as input to the debconf-set-selections command.
- As of Ubuntu 6.10, the `keyboard` option takes X layout names. To use an X keyboard variant, set this option to `layout_variant`, with appropriate values of `layout` and `variant`. For example, `in_guj` selects the Gujarati variant of the Indian layout.
- You may use the **apt-install** command to install packages in `%post --nochroot` scripts (although you might also choose to generate a `%packages` section in a `%pre` script and include it using `%include`). Note that this does not work if the post-installation script is run in the chroot environment.

4.6.2.2. Missing features

As yet, the Ubuntu installer only supports a subset of Kickstart's features. The following is a brief summary of features that are known to be missing:

53

Ubuntu 9.10

- LDAP, Kerberos 5, Hesiod, and Samba authentication.
- The `auth --enablecache` command to enable `nscd`.
- The `bootloader --linear`, `--nolinear`, and `--lba32` options for detailed LILO configuration.
- Upgrades. To upgrade from one Ubuntu release to another, use the facilities provided by `apt` and its frontends.
- Partitioning of multiple drives. Due to current limitations in the partition manager, it is only possible to partition a single drive.
- Using the `device` command to install extra kernel modules.
- Driver disks.
- Firewall configuration.
- Installation from an archive on a local hard disk or from an NFS archive.
- The `lilocheck` command to check for an existing LILO installation.
- Logical Volume Management (LVM) configuration.
- Restrictions of a partition to a particular disk or device, and specifications of the starting or ending cylinder for a partition.
- Checking a partition for bad sectors.
- RAID configuration.
- The `xconfig --monitor` option to use a specified monitor name.
- Most package groups. As special cases, the "Ubuntu Desktop" and "Kubuntu Desktop" groups install the standard Ubuntu or Kubuntu desktop systems respectively, and any group name not containing a space (for example, "ubuntu-desktop") causes packages with the corresponding Task: header in the Packages file to be installed.
- Exclusions in %packages sections are no longer supported as of Ubuntu 6.10, as a casualty of other improvements. You may need to use a %post script instead to remove unnecessary packages.
- Pre-installation scripts and non-chrooted post-installation scripts may only be shell scripts; other interpreters are not available at this point in the installation.

Chapter 5. Booting the Installation System

5.1. Booting the Installer on Intel x86

> **Note**
>
> If you have any other operating systems on your system that you wish to keep (dual boot setup), you should make sure that they have been properly shut down *before* you boot the installer. Installing an operating system while another operating system is in hibernation (has been suspended to disk) could result in loss of, or damage to the state of the suspended operating system which could cause problems when it is rebooted.

> **Warning**
>
> For information on how to boot the graphical installer, see *the section called "The Graphical Installer"*.

5.1.1. Booting from a CD-ROM

The easiest route for most people will be to use an Ubuntu CD. If you have a CD, and if your machine supports booting directly off the CD, great! Simply configure your system for booting off a CD as described in *the section called "Boot Device Selection"*, insert your CD, reboot, and proceed to the next chapter.

Note that certain CD drives may require special drivers, and thus be inaccessible in the early installation stages. If it turns out the standard way of booting off a CD doesn't work for your hardware, revisit this chapter and read about alternate kernels and installation methods which may work for you.

If you have problems booting, see *the section called "Troubleshooting the Installation Process"*.

5.1.2. Booting from Linux Using LILO or GRUB

To boot the installer from hard disk, you must first download and place the needed files as described in *the section called "Preparing Files for Hard Disk Booting"*.

Ubuntu 9.10

If you intend to use the hard drive only for booting and then download everything over the network, you should download the `netboot/ubuntu-installer/i386/initrd.gz` file and its corresponding kernel `netboot/ubuntu-installer/i386/linux`. This will allow you to repartition the hard disk from which you boot the installer, although you should do so with care.

For **LILO**, you will need to configure two essential things in `/etc/lilo.conf`:

- to load the `initrd.gz` installer at boot time;
- have the `vmlinuz` kernel use a RAM disk as its root partition.

Here is a `/etc/lilo.conf` example:

```
image=/boot/newinstall/vmlinuz
      label=newinstall
      initrd=/boot/newinstall/initrd.gz
```

For more details, refer to the initrd(4) and lilo.conf(5) man pages. Now run `lilo` and reboot.

The procedure for **GRUB** is quite similar. Locate your `menu.lst` in the `/boot/grub/` directory (sometimes in the `/boot/boot/grub/`), add the following lines:

```
title  New Install
kernel (hd0,0)/boot/newinstall/vmlinuz
initrd (hd0,0)/boot/newinstall/initrd.gz
```

and reboot.

Note that the value of the **ramdisk_size** may need to be adjusted for the size of the initrd image. From here on, there should be no difference between **GRUB** or **LILO**.

5.1.3. Booting from USB Memory Stick

Let's assume you have prepared everything from *the section called "Boot Device Selection"* and *the section called "Preparing Files for USB Memory Stick Booting"*. Now just plug your USB stick into some free USB connector and reboot the computer. The system should boot up, and you should be presented with the `boot:` prompt. Here you can enter optional boot arguments, or just hit **Enter**.

5.1.4. Booting with TFTP

Booting from the network requires that you have a network connection and a TFTP network boot server (DHCP, RARP, or BOOTP).

The installation method to support network booting is described in *the section called "Preparing Files for TFTP Net Booting"*.

There are various ways to do a TFTP boot on i386.

Installation Guide

5.1.4.1. NIC or Motherboard that support PXE

It could be that your Network Interface Card or Motherboard provides PXE boot functionality. This is a Intel™ re-implementation of TFTP boot. If so, you may be able to configure your BIOS to boot from the network.

5.1.4.2. NIC with Network BootROM

It could be that your Network Interface Card provides TFTP boot functionality.

5.1.4.3. Etherboot

The *etherboot project*[1] provides bootdiskettes and even bootroms that do a TFTPboot.

5.1.5. The Boot Screen

When the installer boots, you should be presented with a friendly graphical screen showing the Ubuntu logo and a menu:

```
Installer boot menu

Install
Graphical install
Advanced options        >
Help

Press ENTER to boot or TAB to edit a menu entry
```

Depending on the installation method you are using, the "Graphical install" option may not be available.

For a normal installation, select either the "Install" or the "Graphical install" entry — using either the arrow keys on your keyboard or by typing the first (highlighted) letter — and press **Enter** to boot the installer.

The "Advanced options" entry gives access to a second menu that allows to boot the installer in expert mode, in rescue mode and for automated installs.

If you wish or need to add any boot parameters for either the installer or the kernel, press **Tab**. This will display the default boot command for the selected menu entry and allow to add additional options. The help screens (see below) list some common possible options. Press **Enter** to boot the installer with your options; pressing **Esc** will return you to the boot menu and undo any changes you made.

Choosing the "Help" entry will result in the first help screen being displayed which gives an overview of all available help screens. Note that it is not possible to return to the boot menu

---

[1] *http://www.etherboot.org/*

after the help screens have been displayed. However, the F3 and F4 help screens list commands that are equivalent to the boot methods listed in the menu. All help screens have a boot prompt at which the boot command can be typed:

```
Press F1 for the help index, or ENTER to boot:
```

At this boot prompt you can either just press **Enter** to boot the installer with default options or enter a specific boot command and, optionally, boot parameters. A number of boot parameters which might be useful can be found on the various help screens. If you do add any parameters to the boot command line, be sure to first type the boot method (the default is `install`) and a space before the first parameter (e.g., `install fb=false`).

> **Note**
>
> The keyboard is assumed to have a default American English layout at this point. This means that if your keyboard has a different (language-specific) layout, the characters that appear on the screen may be different from what you'd expect when you type parameters. Wikipedia has a *schema of the US keyboard layout*[2] which can be used as a reference to find the correct keys to use.

> **Note**
>
> If you are using a system that has the BIOS configured to use serial console, you may not be able to see the initial graphical splash screen upon booting the installer; you may even not see the boot menu. The same can happen if you are installing the system via a remote management device that provides a text interface to the VGA console. Examples of these devices include the text console of Compaq's "integrated Lights Out" (iLO) and HP's "Integrated Remote Assistant" (IRA).
>
> To bypass the graphical boot screen you can either blindly press **Esc** to get a text boot prompt, or (equally blindly) press "H" followed by **Enter** to select the "Help" option described above. After that your keystrokes should be echoed at the prompt. To prevent the installer from using the framebuffer for the rest of the installation, you will also want to add `fb=false` to the boot prompt, as described in the help text.

5.2. Boot Parameters

Boot parameters are Linux kernel parameters which are generally used to make sure that peripherals are dealt with properly. For the most part, the kernel can auto-detect information about your peripherals. However, in some cases you'll have to help the kernel a bit.

---

[2] *http://en.wikipedia.org/wiki/Keymap#US*

Installation Guide

If this is the first time you're booting the system, try the default boot parameters (i.e., don't try setting parameters) and see if it works correctly. It probably will. If not, you can reboot later and look for any special parameters that inform the system about your hardware.

Information on many boot parameters can be found in the *Linux BootPrompt HOWTO*[3], including tips for obscure hardware. This section contains only a sketch of the most salient parameters. Some common gotchas are included below in *the section called "Troubleshooting the Installation Process"*.

When the kernel boots, a message

`Memory:availk/totalk available`

should be emitted early in the process. `total` should match the total amount of RAM, in kilobytes. If this doesn't match the actual amount of RAM you have installed, you need to use the **mem= *ram*** parameter, where `ram` is set to the amount of memory, suffixed with "k" for kilobytes, or "m" for megabytes. For example, both **mem=65536k** and **mem=64m** mean 64MB of RAM.

If you are booting with a serial console, generally the kernel will autodetect this. If you have a videocard (framebuffer) and a keyboard also attached to the computer which you wish to boot via serial console, you may have to pass the **console=*device*** argument to the kernel, where `device` is your serial device, which is usually something like ttyS0.

5.2.1. Ubuntu Installer Parameters

The installation system recognizes a few additional boot parameters[4] which may be useful.

A number of parameters have a "short form" that helps avoid the limitations of the kernel command line options and makes entering the parameters easier. If a parameter has a short form, it will be listed in brackets behind the (normal) long form. Examples in this manual will normally use the short form too.

debconf/priority (priority)

This parameter sets the lowest priority of messages to be displayed.

The default installation uses **priority=high**. This means that both high and critical priority messages are shown, but medium and low priority messages are skipped. If problems are encountered, the installer adjusts the priority as needed.

If you add **priority=medium** as boot parameter, you will be shown the installation menu and gain more control over the installation. When **priority=low** is used, all

---

[3] *http://www.tldp.org/HOWTO/BootPrompt-HOWTO.html*
[4] With current kernels (2.6.9 or newer) you can use 32 command line options and 32 environment options. If these numbers are exceeded, the kernel will panic.

messages are shown (this is equivalent to the *expert* boot method). With `priority=critical`, the installation system will display only critical messages and try to do the right thing without fuss.

DEBIAN_FRONTEND

This boot parameter controls the type of user interface used for the installer. The current possible parameter settings are:

- `DEBIAN_FRONTEND=noninteractive`
- `DEBIAN_FRONTEND=text`
- `DEBIAN_FRONTEND=newt`
- `DEBIAN_FRONTEND=gtk`

The default frontend is `DEBIAN_FRONTEND=newt`. `DEBIAN_FRONTEND=text` may be preferable for serial console installs. Generally, only the `newt` frontend is available on default install media. On architectures that support it, the graphical installer uses the `gtk` frontend.

BOOT_DEBUG

Setting this boot parameter to 2 will cause the installer's boot process to be verbosely logged. Setting it to 3 makes debug shells available at strategic points in the boot process. (Exit the shells to continue the boot process.)

`BOOT_DEBUG=0`

> This is the default.

`BOOT_DEBUG=1`

> More verbose than usual.

`BOOT_DEBUG=2`

> Lots of debugging information.

`BOOT_DEBUG=3`

> Shells are run at various points in the boot process to allow detailed debugging. Exit the shell to continue the boot.

INSTALL_MEDIA_DEV

The value of the parameter is the path to the device to load the Debian installer from. For example, `INSTALL_MEDIA_DEV=/dev/floppy/0`

The boot floppy, which normally scans all floppies it can to find the root floppy, can be overridden by this parameter to only look at the one device.

lowmem

Can be used to force the installer to a lowmem level higher than the one the installer sets by default based on available memory. Possible values are 1 and 2. See also *the section called "Check available memory / low memory mode"*.

debian-installer/framebuffer (fb)

Some architectures use the kernel framebuffer to offer installation in a number of languages. If framebuffer causes a problem on your system you can disable the feature by the parameter `fb=false`. Problem symptoms are error messages about bterm or bogl, a blank screen, or a freeze within a few minutes after starting the install.

The `video=vga16:off` argument may also be used to disable the kernel's use of the framebuffer. Such problems have been reported on a Dell Inspiron with Mobile Radeon card.

debian-installer/theme (theme)

A theme determines how the user interface of the installer looks (colors, icons, etc.). What themes are available differs per frontend. Currently both the newt and gtk frontends only have a "dark" theme that was designed for visually impaired users. Set the theme by booting with `theme= dark`.

netcfg/disable_dhcp

By default, the `debian-installer` automatically probes for network configuration via DHCP. If the probe succeeds, you won't have a chance to review and change the obtained settings. You can get to the manual network setup only in case the DHCP probe fails.

If you have a DHCP server on your local network, but want to avoid it because e.g. it gives wrong answers, you can use the parameter `netcfg/disable_dhcp=true` to prevent configuring the network with DHCP and to enter the information manually.

hw-detect/start_pcmcia

Set to `false` to prevent starting PCMCIA services, if that causes problems. Some laptops are well known for this misbehavior.

disk-detect/dmraid/enable (dmraid)

Set to `true` to enable support for Serial ATA RAID (also called ATA RAID, BIOS RAID or fake RAID) disks in the installer. Note that this support is currently experimental. Additional information can be found on the *Debian Installer Wiki*[5].

---

[5] http://wiki.debian.org/DebianInstaller/

preseed/url (url)
> Specify the url to a preconfiguration file to download and use for automating the install. See *the section called "Automatic Installation"*.

preseed/file (file)
> Specify the path to a preconfiguration file to load for automating the install. See *the section called "Automatic Installation"*.

preseed/interactive
> Set to `true` to display questions even if they have been preseeded. Can be useful for testing or debugging a preconfiguration file. Note that this will have no effect on parameters that are passed as boot parameters, but for those a special syntax can be used. See *the section called "Using preseeding to change default values"* for details.

auto-install/enable (auto)
> Delay questions that are normally asked before preseeding is possible until after the network is configured. See *the section called "Auto mode"* for details about using this to automate installs.

finish-install/keep-consoles
> During installations from serial or management console, the regular virtual consoles (VT1 to VT6) are normally disabled in `/etc/inittab`. Set to `true` to prevent this.

cdrom-detect/eject
> By default, before rebooting, `debian-installer` automatically ejects the optical media used during the installation. This can be unnecessary if the system does not automatically boot off the CD. In some cases it may even be undesirable, for example if the optical drive cannot reinsert the media itself and the user is not there to do it manually. Many slot loading, slim-line, and caddy style drives cannot reload media automatically.
>
> Set to `false` to disable automatic ejection, and be aware that you may need to ensure that the system does not automatically boot from the optical drive after the initial installation.

debian-installer/allow_unauthenticated
> By default the installer requires that repositories be authenticated using a known gpg key. Set to `true` to disable that authentication. **Warning: insecure, not recommended.**

mouse/protocol
> For the gtk frontend (graphical installer), users can set the mouse protocol to be used by setting this parameter. Supported values are[6]: `PS/2`, `IMPS/2`, `MS`, `MS3`, `MouseMan` and `MouseSystems`. In most cases the default protocol should work correctly.

---

[6] See the man page for directfbrc(5) for additional information.

Installation Guide

mouse/device

For the gtk frontend (graphical installer), users can specify the mouse device to be used by setting this parameter. This is mostly useful if the mouse is connected to a serial port (serial mouse). Example: `mouse/device= /dev/ttyS1`.

mouse/left

For the gtk frontend (graphical installer), users can switch the mouse to left-handed operation by setting this parameter to `true`.

directfb/hw-accel

For the gtk frontend (graphical installer), hardware acceleration in directfb is disabled by default. Set this parameter to `true` to enable it.

rescue/enable

Set to `true` to enter rescue mode rather than performing a normal installation. See *the section called "Recovering a Broken System"*.

5.2.1.1. Using boot parameters to answer questions

With some exceptions, a value can be set at the boot prompt for any question asked during the installation, though this is only really useful in specific cases. General instructions how to do this can be found in *the section called "Using boot parameters to preseed questions"*. Some specific examples are listed below.

debian-installer/locale (locale)

Can be used to set both the language and country for the installation. This will only work if the locale is supported in Debian. For example, use `locale=de_CH` to select German as language and Switzerland as country.

anna/choose_modules (modules)

Can be used to automatically load installer components that are not loaded by default. Examples of optional components that may be useful are `openssh-client-udeb` (so you can use **scp** during the installation) and `ppp-udeb` (see *the section called "Installing Ubuntu using PPP over Ethernet (PPPoE)"*).

netcfg/disable_dhcp

Set to `true` if you want to disable DHCP and instead force static network configuration.

mirror/protocol (protocol)

By default the installer will use the http protocol to download files from Debian mirrors and changing that to ftp is not possible during installations at normal priority. By setting

63

tasksel:tasksel/first (tasks)

> this parameter to `ftp`, you can force the installer to use that protocol instead. Note that you cannot select an ftp mirror from a list, you have to enter the hostname manually.

> Can be used to select tasks that are not available from the interactive task list, such as the `kde-desktop` task. See *the section called "Selecting and Installing Software"* for additional information.

5.2.1.2. Passing parameters to kernel modules

If drivers are compiled into the kernel, you can pass parameters to them as described in the kernel documentation. However, if drivers are compiled as modules and because kernel modules are loaded a bit differently during an installation than when booting an installed system, it is not possible to pass parameters to modules as you would normally do. Instead, you need to use a special syntax recognized by the installer which will then make sure that the parameters are saved in the proper configuration files and will thus be used when the modules are actually loaded. The parameters will also be propagated automatically to the configuration for the installed system.

Note that it is now quite rare that parameters need to be passed to modules. In most cases the kernel will be able to probe the hardware present in a system and set good defaults that way. However, in some situations it may still be needed to set parameters manually.

The syntax to use to set parameters for modules is:

```
module_name.parameter_name=value
```

If you need to pass multiple parameters to the same or different modules, just repeat this. For example, to set an old 3Com network interface card to use the BNC (coax) connector and IRQ 10, you would pass:

```
3c509.xcvr=3 3c509.irq=10
```

5.2.1.3. Blacklisting kernel modules

Sometimes it may be necessary to blacklist a module to prevent it from being loaded automatically by the kernel and udev. One reason could be that a particular module causes problems with your hardware. The kernel also sometimes lists two different drivers for the same device. This can cause the device to not work correctly if the drivers conflict or if the wrong driver is loaded first.

You can blacklist a module using the following syntax: `module_name.blacklist=yes`. This will cause the module to be blacklisted in `/etc/modprobe.d/blacklist.local` both during the installation and for the installed system.

Installation Guide

Note that a module may still be loaded by the installation system itself. You can prevent that from happening by running the installation in expert mode and unselecting the module from the list of modules displayed during the hardware detection phases.

5.3. Troubleshooting the Installation Process

5.3.1. CD-ROM Reliability

Sometimes, especially with older CD-ROM drives, the installer may fail to boot from a CD-ROM. The installer may also — even after booting successfully from CD-ROM — fail to recognize the CD-ROM or return errors while reading from it during the installation.

There are many different possible causes for these problems. We can only list some common issues and provide general suggestions on how to deal with them. The rest is up to you.

There are two very simple things that you should try first.

- If the CD-ROM does not boot, check that it was inserted correctly and that it is not dirty.
- If the installer fails to recognize a CD-ROM, try just running the option Detect and mount CD-ROM a second time. Some DMA related issues with older CD-ROM drives are known to be resolved in this way.

If this does not work, then try the suggestions in the subsections below. Most, but not all, suggestions discussed there are valid for both CD-ROM and DVD, but we'll use the term CD-ROM for simplicity.

If you cannot get the installation working from CD-ROM, try one of the other installation methods that are available.

5.3.1.1. Common issues

- Some older CD-ROM drives do not support reading from discs that were burned at high speeds using a modern CD writer.
- If your system boots correctly from the CD-ROM, it does not necessarily mean that Linux also supports the CD-ROM (or, more correctly, the controller that your CD-ROM drive is connected to).
- Some older CD-ROM drives do not work correctly if "direct memory access" (DMA) is enabled.

5.3.1.2. How to investigate and maybe solve issues

If the CD-ROM fails to boot, try the suggestions listed below.

- Check that your BIOS actually supports booting from CD-ROM (older systems possibly don't) and that your CD-ROM drive supports the media you are using.

- If you downloaded an iso image, check that the md5sum of that image matches the one listed for the image in the MD5SUMS file that should be present in the same location as where you downloaded the image from.

  ```
  $ md5sum debian-testing-i386-netinst.iso
  a20391b12f7ff22ef705cee4059c6b92  debian-testing-i386-netinst.iso
  ```

  Next, check that the md5sum of the burned CD-ROM matches as well. The following command should work. It uses the size of the image to read the correct number of bytes from the CD-ROM.

  ```
  $ dd if=/dev/cdrom | \
  > head -c `stat --format=%s debian-testing-i386-netinst.iso` | \
  > md5sum
  a20391b12f7ff22ef705cee4059c6b92  -
  262668+0 records in
  262668+0 records out
  134486016 bytes (134 MB) copied, 97.474 seconds, 1.4 MB/s
  ```

If, after the installer has been booted successfully, the CD-ROM is not detected, sometimes simply trying again may solve the problem. If you have more than one CD-ROM drive, try changing the CD-ROM to the other drive. If that does not work or if the CD-ROM is recognized but there are errors when reading from it, try the suggestions listed below. Some basic knowledge of Linux is required for this. To execute any of the commands, you should first switch to the second virtual console (VT2) and activate the shell there.

- Switch to VT4 or view the contents of /var/log/syslog (use **nano** as editor) to check for any specific error messages. After that, also check the output of **dmesg**.

- Check in the output of **dmesg** if your CD-ROM drive was recognized. You should see something like (the lines do not necessarily have to be consecutive):

  ```
  Probing IDE interface ide1...
  hdc: TOSHIBA DVD-ROM SD-R6112, ATAPI CD/DVD-ROM drive
  ide1 at 0x170-0x177,0x376 on irq 15
  hdc: ATAPI 24X DVD-ROM DVD-R CD-R/RW drive, 2048kB Cache, UDMA(33)
  Uniform CD-ROM driver Revision: 3.20
  ```

  If you don't see something like that, chances are the controller your CD-ROM is connected to was not recognized or may be not supported at all. If you know what driver is needed for the controller, you can try loading it manually using **modprobe**.

- Check that there is a device node for your CD-ROM drive under /dev/. In the example above, this would be /dev/hdc. There should also be a /dev/cdrom.

- Use the **mount** command to check if the CD-ROM is already mounted; if not, try mounting it manually:

  ```
  $ mount /dev/hdc /cdrom
  ```

  Check if there are any error messages after that command.

Installation Guide

- Check if DMA is currently enabled:

  ```
  $ cd /proc/ide/hdc
  $ grep using_dma settings
  using_dma       1       0       1       rw
  ```

  A "1" in the first column after `using_dma` means it is enabled. If it is, try disabling it:

  ```
  $ echo -n "using_dma:0" >settings
  ```

  Make sure that you are in the directory for the device that corresponds to your CD-ROM drive.

- If there are any problems during the installation, try checking the integrity of the CD-ROM using the option near the bottom of the installer's main menu. This option can also be used as a general test if the CD-ROM can be read reliably.

5.3.2. Boot Configuration

If you have problems and the kernel hangs during the boot process, doesn't recognize peripherals you actually have, or drives are not recognized properly, the first thing to check is the boot parameters, as discussed in *the section called "Boot Parameters"*.

Often, problems can be solved by removing add-ons and peripherals, and then trying booting again. Internal modems, sound cards, and Plug-n-Play devices can be especially problematic.

If you have a large amount of memory installed in your machine, more than 512M, and the installer hangs when booting the kernel, you may need to include a boot argument to limit the amount of memory the kernel sees, such as `mem=512m`.

5.3.3. Common Intel x86 Installation Problems

There are some common installation problems that can be solved or avoided by passing certain boot parameters to the installer.

Some systems have floppies with "inverted DCLs". If you receive errors reading from the floppy, even when you know the floppy is good, try the parameter `floppy=thinkpad`.

On some systems, such as the IBM PS/1 or ValuePoint (which have ST-506 disk drivers), the IDE drive may not be properly recognized. Again, try it first without the parameters and see if the IDE drive is recognized properly. If not, determine your drive geometry (cylinders, heads, and sectors), and use the parameter `hd=cylinders,heads,sectors`.

If you have a very old machine, and the kernel hangs after saying `Checking 'hlt' instruction...`, then you should try the `no-hlt` boot argument, which disables this test.

Some systems (especially laptops) that have a native resolution that is not a 4:3 ratio (i.e. not for example 800x600 or 1024x768) may have a blank display after the installer has been booted. In that case adding the boot parameter `vga=788`[7] may help. If that does not work, try adding the boot parameter `fb=false`.

If your screen begins to show a weird picture while the kernel boots, eg. pure white, pure black or colored pixel garbage, your system may contain a problematic video card which does not switch to the framebuffer mode properly. Then you can use the boot parameter `fb=false` to disable the framebuffer console. Only a reduced set of languages will be available during the installation due to limited console features. See *the section called "Boot Parameters"* for details.

5.3.3.1. System Freeze During the PCMCIA Configuration Phase

Some laptop models produced by Dell are known to crash when PCMCIA device detection tries to access some hardware addresses. Other laptops may display similar problems. If you experience such a problem and you don't need PCMCIA support during the installation, you can disable PCMCIA using the `hw-detect/start_pcmcia=false` boot parameter. You can then configure PCMCIA after the installation is completed and exclude the resource range causing the problems.

Alternatively, you can boot the installer in expert mode. You will then be asked to enter the resource range options your hardware needs. For example, if you have one of the Dell laptops mentioned above, you should enter `exclude port 0x800-0x8ff` here. There is also a list of some common resource range options in the *System resource settings section of the PCMCIA HOWTO*[8]. Note that you have to omit the commas, if any, when you enter this value in the installer.

5.3.3.2. System Freeze while Loading USB Modules

The kernel normally tries to install USB modules and the USB keyboard driver in order to support some non-standard USB keyboards. However, there are some broken USB systems where the driver hangs on loading. A possible workaround may be disabling the USB controller in your mainboard BIOS setup. Another option is passing the `nousb` parameter at the boot prompt.

5.3.4. Interpreting the Kernel Startup Messages

During the boot sequence, you may see many messages in the form `can't find` *something*, or *something* `not present`, `can't initialize` *something*, or even this

---

[7] The parameter `vga=788` will activate the VESA framebuffer with a resolution of 800x600. This will probably work, but may not be the optimal resolution for your system. A list of supported resolutions can be obtained by using `vga=ask`, but you should be aware that list may not be complete.
[8] *http://pcmcia-cs.sourceforge.net/ftp/doc/PCMCIA-HOWTO-1.html#ss1.12*

Installation Guide

driver release depends on something. Most of these messages are harmless. You see them because the kernel for the installation system is built to run on computers with many different peripheral devices. Obviously, no one computer will have every possible peripheral device, so the operating system may emit a few complaints while it looks for peripherals you don't own. You may also see the system pause for a while. This happens when it is waiting for a device to respond, and that device is not present on your system. If you find the time it takes to boot the system unacceptably long, you can create a custom kernel later (see *the section called "Compiling a New Kernel"*).

5.3.5. Reporting Installation Problems

If you get through the initial boot phase but cannot complete the install, the menu option Save debug logs may be helpful. It lets you store system error logs and configuration information from the installer to a floppy, or download them using a web browser. This information may provide clues as to what went wrong and how to fix it. If you are submitting a bug report, you may want to attach this information to the bug report.

Other pertinent installation messages may be found in `/var/log/` during the installation, and `/var/log/installer/` after the computer has been booted into the installed system.

5.3.6. Submitting Installation Reports

If you still have problems, please submit an installation report. We also encourage installation reports to be sent even if the installation is successful, so that we can get as much information as possible on the largest number of hardware configurations.

Note that your installation report will be published in the Debian Bug Tracking System (BTS) and forwarded to a public mailing list. Make sure that you use an e-mail address that you do not mind being made public.

If you have a working Ubuntu system, the easiest way to send an installation report is to install the `installation-report` and `reportbug` packages (**aptitude install installation-report reportbug**), configure `reportbug` as explained in *the section called "Sending E-Mails Outside The System"*, and run the command **reportbug installation-reports**.

Alternatively you can use this template when filling out installation reports, and send the report to `<ubuntu-users@lists.ubuntu.com>`.

```
Package: installation-reports

Boot method: <How did you boot the installer? CD? floppy? network?>
Image version: <Full URL to image you downloaded is best>
Date: <Date and time of the install>

Machine: <Description of machine (eg, IBM Thinkpad R32)>
Processor:
```

69

Ubuntu 9.10

```
Memory:
Partitions: <df -Tl will do; the raw partition table is preferred>

Output of lspci -knn (or lspci -nn):

Base System Installation Checklist:
[O] = OK, [E] = Error (please elaborate below), [ ] = didn't try it

Initial boot:              [ ]
Detect network card:       [ ]
Configure network:         [ ]
Detect CD:                 [ ]
Load installer modules:    [ ]
Detect hard drives:        [ ]
Partition hard drives:     [ ]
Install base system:       [ ]
Clock/timezone setup:      [ ]
User/password setup:       [ ]
Install tasks:             [ ]
Install boot loader:       [ ]
Overall install:           [ ]

Comments/Problems:

<Description of the install, in prose, and any thoughts, comments
     and ideas you had during the initial install.>
```

In the bug report, describe what the problem is, including the last visible kernel messages in the event of a kernel hang. Describe the steps that you did which brought the system into the problem state.

Chapter 6.
Using the Ubuntu Installer

6.1. How the Installer Works

The Ubuntu Installer (based on the Debian Installer, and so often called simply `debian-installer`) consists of a number of special-purpose components to perform each installation task. Each component performs its task, asking the user questions as necessary to do its job. The questions themselves are given priorities, and the priority of questions to be asked is set when the installer is started.

When a default installation is performed, only essential (high priority) questions will be asked. This results in a highly automated installation process with little user interaction. Components are automatically run in sequence; which components are run depends mainly on the installation method you use and on your hardware. The installer will use default values for questions that are not asked.

If there is a problem, the user will see an error screen, and the installer menu may be shown in order to select some alternative action. If there are no problems, the user will never see the installer menu, but will simply answer questions for each component in turn. Serious error notifications are set to priority "critical" so the user will always be notified.

Some of the defaults that the installer uses can be influenced by passing boot arguments when `debian-installer` is started. If, for example, you wish to force static network configuration (DHCP is used by default if available), you could add the boot parameter `netcfg/disable_dhcp=true`. See *the section called "Ubuntu Installer Parameters"* for available options.

Power users may be more comfortable with a menu-driven interface, where each step is controlled by the user rather than the installer performing each step automatically in sequence. To use the installer in a manual, menu-driven way, add the boot argument `priority=medium`.

If your hardware requires you to pass options to kernel modules as they are installed, you will need to start the installer in "expert" mode. This can be done by either using the **expert** command to start the installer or by adding the boot argument `priority=low`. Expert mode gives you full control over `debian-installer`.

For this architecture the `debian-installer` supports two different user interfaces: a character-based one and a graphical one. The character-based interface is used by default unless you selected the "Graphical install" option in the initial boot menu. For more information about the graphical installer, please refer to *the section called "The Graphical Installer"*.

In the character-based environment the use of a mouse is not supported. Here are the keys you can use to navigate within the various dialogs. The **Tab** or **right** arrow keys move "forward", and the **Shift**+ **Tab** or **left** arrow keys move "backward" between displayed buttons and selections. The **up** and **down** arrow select different items within a scrollable list, and also scroll the list itself. In addition, in long lists, you can type a letter to cause the list to scroll directly to the section with items starting with the letter you typed and use **Pg-Up** and **Pg-Down** to scroll the list in sections. The **space bar** selects an item such as a checkbox. Use **Enter** to activate choices.

Error messages and logs are redirected to the fourth console. You can access this console by pressing **Left Alt**+ **F4** (hold the left **Alt** key while pressing the **F4** function key); get back to the main installer process with **Left Alt**+ **F1**.

These messages can also be found in `/var/log/syslog`. After installation, this log is copied to `/var/log/installer/syslog` on your new system. Other installation messages may be found in `/var/log/` during the installation, and `/var/log/installer/` after the computer has been booted into the installed system.

6.2. Components Introduction

Here is a list of installer components with a brief description of each component's purpose. Details you might need to know about using a particular component are in *the section called "Using Individual Components"*.

main-menu

Shows the list of components to the user during installer operation, and starts a component when it is selected. Main-menu's questions are set to priority medium, so if your priority is set to high or critical (high is the default), you will not see the menu. On the other hand, if there is an error which requires your intervention, the question priority may be downgraded temporarily to allow you to resolve the problem, and in that case the menu may appear.

You can get to the main menu by selecting the **Go Back** button repeatedly to back all the way out of the currently running component.

localechooser

Allows the user to select localization options for the installation and the installed system: language, country and locales. The installer will display messages in the selected language, unless the translation for that language is not complete in which case some messages may be shown in English.

kbd-chooser

Shows a list of keyboards, from which the user chooses the model which matches his own.

hw-detect

Automatically detects most of the system's hardware, including network cards, disk drives, and PCMCIA.

cdrom-detect

Looks for and mounts an Ubuntu installation CD.

netcfg

Configures the computer's network connections so it can communicate over the internet.

iso-scan

Searches for ISO images (`.iso` files) on hard drives.

choose-mirror

Presents a list of Ubuntu archive mirrors. The user may choose the source of his installation packages.

cdrom-checker

Checks integrity of a CD-ROM. This way, the user may assure him/herself that the installation CD-ROM was not corrupted.

lowmem

Lowmem tries to detect systems with low memory and then does various tricks to remove unnecessary parts of `debian-installer` from the memory (at the cost of some features).

anna

Anna's Not Nearly APT. Installs packages which have been retrieved from the chosen mirror or CD.

clock-setup

Updates the system clock and determines whether the clock is set to UTC or not.

tzsetup

Selects the time zone, based on the location selected earlier.

partman

Allows the user to partition disks attached to the system, create file systems on the selected partitions, and attach them to the mountpoints. Included are also interesting features like a fully automatic mode or LVM support. This is the preferred partitioning tool in Ubuntu.

lvmcfg

Helps the user with the configuration of the *LVM* (Logical Volume Manager).

mdcfg

Allows the user to set up Software *RAID* (Redundant Array of Inexpensive Disks). This Software RAID is usually superior to the cheap IDE (pseudo hardware) RAID controllers found on newer motherboards.

base-installer

Installs the most basic set of packages which would allow the computer to operate under Linux when rebooted.

user-setup

Sets up the root password, and adds a non-root user.

apt-setup

Configures apt, mostly automatically, based on what media the installer is running from.

pkgsel

Uses `tasksel` to select and install additional software.

os-prober

Detects currently installed operating systems on the computer and passes this information to the bootloader-installer, which may offer you an ability to add discovered operating systems to the bootloader's start menu. This way the user could easily choose at the boot time which operating system to start.

bootloader-installer

The various bootloader installers each install a boot loader program on the hard disk, which is necessary for the computer to start up using Linux without using a floppy or CD-ROM. Many boot loaders allow the user to choose an alternate operating system each time the computer boots.

shell

Allows the user to execute a shell from the menu, or in the second console.

Installation Guide

save-logs

> Provides a way for the user to record information on a floppy disk, network, hard disk, or other media when trouble is encountered, in order to accurately report installer software problems to Ubuntu developers later.

6.3. Using Individual Components

In this section we will describe each installer component in detail. The components have been grouped into stages that should be recognizable for users. They are presented in the order they appear during the install. Note that not all modules will be used for every installation; which modules are actually used depends on the installation method you use and on your hardware.

6.3.1. Setting up Ubuntu Installer and Hardware Configuration

Let's assume the Ubuntu Installer has booted and you are facing its first screen. At this time, the capabilities of debian-installer are still quite limited. It doesn't know much about your hardware, preferred language, or even the task it should perform. Don't worry. Because debian-installer is quite clever, it can automatically probe your hardware, locate the rest of its components and upgrade itself to a capable installation system. However, you still need to help debian-installer with some information it can't determine automatically (like selecting your preferred language, keyboard layout or desired network mirror).

You will notice that debian-installer performs *hardware detection* several times during this stage. The first time is targeted specifically at the hardware needed to load installer components (e.g. your CD-ROM or network card). As not all drivers may be available during this first run, hardware detection needs to be repeated later in the process.

During hardware detection debian-installer checks if any of the drivers for the hardware devices in your system require firmware to be loaded. If any firmware is requested but unavailable, a dialog will be displayed that allows the missing firmware to be loaded from a removable medium. See *the section called "Loading Missing Firmware"* for further details.

6.3.1.1. Check available memory / low memory mode

One of the first things debian-installer does, is to check available memory. If the available memory is limited, this component will make some changes in the installation process which hopefully will allow you to install Ubuntu on your system.

The first measure taken to reduce memory consumption by the installer is to disable translations, which means that the installation can only be done in English. Of course, you can still localize the installed system after the installation has completed.

If that is not sufficient, the installer will further reduce memory consumption by loading only those components essential to complete a basic installation. This reduces the functionality of the installation system. You will be given the opportunity to load additional components manually, but you should be aware that each component you select will use additional memory and thus may cause the installation to fail.

If the installer runs in low memory mode, it is recommended to create a relatively large swap partition (64–128MB). The swap partition will be used as virtual memory and thus increases the amount of memory available to the system. The installer will activate the swap partition as early as possible in the installation process. Note that heavy use of swap will reduce performance of your system and may lead to high disk activity.

Despite these measures, it is still possible that your system freezes, that unexpected errors occur or that processes are killed by the kernel because the system runs out of memory (which will result in "Out of memory" messages on VT4 and in the syslog).

For example, it has been reported that creating a big ext3 file system fails in low memory mode when there is insufficient swap space. If a larger swap doesn't help, try creating the file system as ext2 (which is an essential component of the installer) instead. It is possible to change an ext2 partition to ext3 after the installation.

It is possible to force the installer to use a higher lowmem level than the one based on available memory by using the boot parameter "lowmem" as described in *the section called "Ubuntu Installer Parameters"*.

6.3.1.2. Selecting Localization Options

In most cases the first questions you will be asked concern the selection of localization options to be used both for the installation and for the installed system. The localization options consist of language, country and locales.

The language you choose will be used for the rest of the installation process, provided a translation of the different dialogs is available. If no valid translation is available for the selected language, the installer will default to English.

The selected country will be used later in the installation process to pick the default timezone and an Ubuntu mirror appropriate for your geographic location. Language and country together will be used to set the default locale for your system and to help select your keyboard.

You will first be asked to select your preferred language. The language names are listed both in English (left side) and in the language itself (right side); the names on the right side are also shown in the proper script for the language. The list is sorted on the English names. At the top of the list is an extra option that allows you to select the "C" locale instead of a language. Choosing the "C" locale will result in the installation proceding in English; the installed system will have no localization support as the `locales` package will not be installed.

If you selected a language that is recognized as an official language for more than one country[1], you will be shown a list of only those countries. To select a country that is not in that list, choose Other (the last option). You will then be presented with a list of continents; selecting a continent will lead to a list of relevant countries on that continent.

If the language has only one country associated with it, that country will be selected automatically. In that case it is only possible to select a different country by first lowering the debconf priority to medium, followed by revisiting the language selection option in the main menu of the installer.

A default locale will be selected based on the selected language and country. If you are installing at medium or low priority, you will have the option of selecting a different default locale and of selecting additional locales to be generated for the installed system.

6.3.1.3. Choosing a Keyboard

Keyboards are often tailored to the characters used in a language. Select a layout that conforms to the keyboard you are using, or select something close if the keyboard layout you want isn't represented. Once the system installation is complete, you'll be able to select a keyboard layout from a wider range of choices (run **kbdconfig** as root after you have completed the installation).

Move the highlight to the keyboard selection you desire and press **Enter**. Use the arrow keys to move the highlight — they are in the same place in all national language keyboard layouts, so they are independent of the keyboard configuration. An 'extended' keyboard is one with **F1** through **F10** keys along the top row.

6.3.1.4. Looking for the Ubuntu Installer ISO Image

When installing via the *hd-media* method, there will be a moment where you need to find and mount the Ubuntu Installer iso image in order to get the rest of the installation files. The component **iso-scan** does exactly this.

At first, **iso-scan** automatically mounts all block devices (e.g. partitions) which have some known filesystem on them and sequentially searches for filenames ending with `.iso` (or `.ISO` for that matter). Beware that the first attempt scans only files in the root directory and in the first level of subdirectories (i.e. it finds `/whatever.iso`, `/data/whatever.iso`, but not `/data/tmp/ whatever.iso`). After an iso image has been found, **iso-scan** checks its

---

[1] In technical terms: where multiple locales exist for that language with differing country codes.

Ubuntu 9.10

content to determine if the image is a valid Ubuntu iso image or not. In the former case we are done, in the latter **iso-scan** seeks for another image.

In case the previous attempt to find an installer iso image fails, **iso-scan** will ask you whether you would like to perform a more thorough search. This pass doesn't just look into the topmost directories, but really traverses whole filesystem.

If **iso-scan** does not discover your installer iso image, reboot back to your original operating system and check if the image is named correctly (ending in .iso), if it is placed on a filesystem recognizable by debian-installer, and if it is not corrupted (verify the checksum). Experienced Unix users could do this without rebooting on the second console.

6.3.1.5. Configuring the Network

As you enter this step, if the system detects that you have more than one network device, you'll be asked to choose which device will be your *primary* network interface, i.e. the one which you want to use for installation. The other interfaces won't be configured at this time. You may configure additional interfaces after installation is complete; see the interfaces(5) man page.

By default, debian-installer tries to configure your computer's network automatically via DHCP. If the DHCP probe succeeds, you are done. If the probe fails, it may be caused by many factors ranging from unplugged network cable, to a misconfigured DHCP setup. Or maybe you don't have a DHCP server in your local network at all. For further explanation, check the error messages on the fourth console. In any case, you will be asked if you want to retry, or if you want to perform a manual setup. DHCP servers are sometimes really slow in their responses, so if you are sure everything is in place, try again.

The manual network setup in turn asks you a number of questions about your network, notably IP address, Netmask, Gateway, Name server addresses, and a Hostname. Moreover, if you have a wireless network interface, you will be asked to provide your Wireless ESSID and a WEP key. Fill in the answers from *the section called "Information You Will Need"*.

> **Note**
>
> Some technical details you might, or might not, find handy: the program assumes the network IP address is the bitwise-AND of your system's IP address and your netmask. The default broadcast address is calculated as the bitwise OR of your system's IP address with the bitwise negation of the netmask. It will also guess your gateway. If you can't find any of these answers, use the offered defaults — if necessary, you can change them by editing /etc/network/interfaces once the system has been installed.

Installation Guide

6.3.1.6. Configuring the Clock

The installer will first attempt to connect to a time server on the Internet (using the *NTP* protocol) in order to correctly set the system time. If this does not succeed, the installer will assume the time and date obtained from the system clock when the installation system was booted are correct. It is not possible to manually set the system time during the installation process.

Depending on the location selected earlier in the installation process, you may be shown a list of timezones relevant for that location. If your location has only one time zone, you will not be asked anything and the system will assume that time zone.

If for some reason you wish to set a time zone for the installed system that does *not* match the selected location, there are two options.

1. The simplest option is to just select a different timezone after the installation has been completed and you've booted into the new system. The command to do this is:
   ```
   # dpkg-reconfigure tzdata
   ```
2. Alternatively, the time zone can be set at the very start of the installation by passing the parameter **time/zone=***value* when you boot the installation system. The value should of course be a valid time zone, for example **Europe/London** or **UTC** .

For automated installations the time zone can also be set using preseeding.

6.3.2. Partitioning and Mount Point Selection

At this time, after hardware detection has been executed a final time, debian-installer should be at its full strength, customized for the user's needs and ready to do some real work. As the title of this section indicates, the main task of the next few components lies in partitioning your disks, creating filesystems, assigning mountpoints and optionally configuring closely related options like RAID, LVM or encrypted devices.

If you are uncomfortable with partitioning, or just want to know more details, see *Appendix C, Partitioning for Ubuntu*.

First you will be given the opportunity to automatically partition either an entire drive, or available free space on a drive. This is also called "guided" partitioning. If you do not want to autopartition, choose Manual from the menu.

6.3.2.1. Guided Partitioning

If you choose guided partitioning, you may have three options: to create partitions directly on the hard disk (classic method), or to create them using Logical Volume Management (LVM), or to create them using encrypted LVM[2].

---

[2] The installer will encrypt the LVM volume group using a 256 bit AES key and makes use of the kernel's "dm-crypt" support.

> **Note**
>
> The option to use (encrypted) LVM may not be available on all architectures.

When using LVM or encrypted LVM, the installer will create most partitions inside one big partition; the advantage of this method is that partitions inside this big partition can be resized relatively easily later. In the case of encrypted LVM the big partition will not be readable without knowing a special key phrase, thus providing extra security of your (personal) data.

When using encrypted LVM, the installer will also automatically erase the disk by writing random data to it. This further improves security (as it makes it impossible to tell which parts of the disk are in use and also makes sure that any traces of previous installations are erased), but may take some time depending on the size of your disk.

> **Note**
>
> If you choose guided partitioning using LVM or encrypted LVM, some changes in the partition table will need to be written to the selected disk while LVM is being set up. These changes effectively erase all data that is currently on the selected hard disk and you will not be able to undo them later. However, the installer will ask you to confirm these changes before they are written to disk.

If you choose guided partitioning (either classic or using (encrypted) LVM) for a whole disk, you will first be asked to select the disk you want to use. Check that all your disks are listed and, if you have several disks, make sure you select the correct one. The order they are listed in may differ from what you are used to. The size of the disks may help to identify them.

Any data on the disk you select will eventually be lost, but you will always be asked to confirm any changes before they are written to the disk. If you have selected the classic method of partitioning, you will be able to undo any changes right until the end; when using (encrypted) LVM this is not possible.

Next, you will be able to choose from the schemes listed in the table below. All schemes have their pros and cons, some of which are discussed in *Appendix C, Partitioning for Ubuntu*. If you are unsure, choose the first one. Bear in mind that guided partitioning needs a certain minimal amount of free space to operate with. If you don't give it at least about 1GB of space (depends on chosen scheme), guided partitioning will fail.

Partitioning scheme	Minimum space	Created partitions
All files in one partition	600MB	/, swap
Separate /home partition	500MB	/, /home, swap
Separate /home, /usr, /var and /tmp partitions	1GB	/, /home, /usr, /var, /tmp, swap

Installation Guide

If you choose guided partitioning using (encrypted) LVM, the installer will also create a separate /boot partition. The other partitions, including the swap partition, will be created inside the LVM partition.

After selecting a scheme, the next screen will show your new partition table, including information on whether and how partitions will be formatted and where they will be mounted.

The list of partitions might look like this:

```
IDE1 master (hda)  - 6.4 GB WDC AC36400L
     #1 primary    16.4 MB  B f ext2        /boot
     #2 primary   551.0 MB      swap        swap
     #3 primary     5.8 GB      ntfs
        pri/log     8.2 MB      FREE SPACE

IDE1 slave (hdb)  - 80.0 GB ST380021A
     #1 primary    15.9 MB      ext3
     #2 primary   996.0 MB      fat16
     #3 primary     3.9 GB      xfs         /home
     #5 logical     6.0 GB    f ext3        /
     #6 logical     1.0 GB    f ext3        /var
     #7 logical   498.8 MB      ext3
     #8 logical   551.5 MB      swap        swap
     #9 logical    65.8 GB      ext2
```

This example shows two IDE harddrives divided into several partitions; the first disk has some free space. Each partition line consists of the partition number, its type, size, optional flags, file system, and mountpoint (if any). Note: this particular setup cannot be created using guided partitioning but it does show possible variation that can be achieved using manual partitioning.

This concludes the guided partitioning. If you are satisfied with the generated partition table, you can choose Finish partitioning and write changes to disk from the menu to implement the new partition table (as described at the end of this section). If you are not happy, you can choose to Undo changes to partitions and run guided partitioning again, or modify the proposed changes as described below for manual partitioning.

6.3.2.2. Manual Partitioning

A similar screen to the one shown just above will be displayed if you choose manual partitioning except that your existing partition table will be shown and without the mount points. How to manually set up your partition table and the usage of partitions by your new Ubuntu system will be covered in the remainder of this section.

If you select a pristine disk which has neither partitions nor free space on it, you will be asked if a new partition table should be created (this is needed so you can create new partitions). After this, a new line entitled "FREE SPACE" should appear in the table under the selected disk.

If you select some free space, you will have the opportunity to create a new partition. You will have to answer a quick series of questions about its size, type (primary or logical), and location (beginning or end of the free space). After this, you will be presented with a detailed overview of your new partition. The main setting is Use as:, which determines if the partition will have a file system on it, or be used for swap, software RAID, LVM, an encrypted file system, or not be used at all. Other settings include mountpoint, mount options, and bootable flag; which settings are shown depends on how the partition is to be used. If you don't like the preselected defaults, feel free to change them to your liking. E.g. by selecting the option Use as:, you can choose a different filesystem for this partition, including options to use the partition for swap, software RAID, LVM, or not use it at all. Another nice feature is the ability to copy data from an existing partition onto this one. When you are satisfied with your new partition, select Done setting up the partition and you will return to **partman**'s main screen.

If you decide you want to change something about your partition, simply select the partition, which will bring you to the partition configuration menu. This is the same screen as is used when creating a new partition, so you can change the same settings. One thing that may not be very obvious at a first glance is that you can resize the partition by selecting the item displaying the size of the partition. Filesystems known to work are at least fat16, fat32, ext2, ext3 and swap. This menu also allows you to delete a partition.

Be sure to create at least two partitions: one for the *root* filesystem (which must be mounted as /) and one for *swap*. If you forget to mount the root filesystem, **partman** won't let you continue until you correct this issue.

Capabilities of **partman** can be extended with installer modules, but are dependent on your system's architecture. So if you can't see all promised goodies, check if you have loaded all required modules (e.g. `partman-ext3`, `partman-xfs`, or `partman-lvm`).

After you are satisfied with partitioning, select Finish partitioning and write changes to disk from the partitioning menu. You will be presented with a summary of changes made to the disks and asked to confirm that the filesystems should be created as requested.

6.3.2.3. Configuring Multidisk Devices (Software RAID)

If you have more than one harddrive[3] in your computer, you can use **mdcfg** to set up your drives for increased performance and/or better reliability of your data. The result is called *Multidisk Device* (or after its most famous variant *software RAID*).

---

[3] To be honest, you can construct an MD device even from partitions residing on single physical drive, but that won't give any benefits.

Installation Guide

MD is basically a bunch of partitions located on different disks and combined together to form a *logical* device. This device can then be used like an ordinary partition (i.e. in **partman** you can format it, assign a mountpoint, etc.).

What benefits this brings depends on the type of MD device you are creating. Currently supported are:

RAID0

Is mainly aimed at performance. RAID0 splits all incoming data into *stripes* and distributes them equally over each disk in the array. This can increase the speed of read/write operations, but when one of the disks fails, you will lose *everything* (part of the information is still on the healthy disk(s), the other part *was* on the failed disk).

The typical use for RAID0 is a partition for video editing.

RAID1

Is suitable for setups where reliability is the first concern. It consists of several (usually two) equally-sized partitions where every partition contains exactly the same data. This essentially means three things. First, if one of your disks fails, you still have the data mirrored on the remaining disks. Second, you can use only a fraction of the available capacity (more precisely, it is the size of the smallest partition in the RAID). Third, file-reads are load-balanced among the disks, which can improve performance on a server, such as a file server, that tends to be loaded with more disk reads than writes.

Optionally you can have a spare disk in the array which will take the place of the failed disk in the case of failure.

RAID5

Is a good compromise between speed, reliability and data redundancy. RAID5 splits all incoming data into stripes and distributes them equally on all but one disk (similar to RAID0). Unlike RAID0, RAID5 also computes *parity* information, which gets written on the remaining disk. The parity disk is not static (that would be called RAID4), but is changing periodically, so the parity information is distributed equally on all disks. When one of the disks fails, the missing part of information can be computed from remaining data and its parity. RAID5 must consist of at least three active partitions. Optionally you can have a spare disk in the array which will take the place of the failed disk in the case of failure.

As you can see, RAID5 has a similar degree of reliability to RAID1 while achieving less redundancy. On the other hand, it might be a bit slower on write operations than RAID0 due to computation of parity information.

RAID6

Is similar to RAID5 except that it uses two parity devices instead of one.

A RAID6 array can survive up to two disk failures.

RAID10

RAID10 combines striping (as in RAID0) and mirroring (as in RAID1). It creates n copies of incoming data and distributes them across the partitions so that none of the copies of the same data are on the same device. The default value of n is 2, but it can be set to something else in expert mode. The number of partitions used must be at least n. RAID10 has different layouts for distributing the copies. The default is near copies. Near copies have all of the copies at about the same offset on all of the disks. Far copies have the copies at different offsets on the disks. Offset copies copy the stripe, not the individual copies.

RAID10 can be used to achieve reliability and redundancy without the drawback of having to calculate parity.

To sum it up:

Type	Minimum Devices	Spare Device	Survives disk failure?	Available Space
RAID0	2	no	no	Size of the smallest partition multiplied by number of devices in RAID
RAID1	2	optional	yes	Size of the smallest partition in RAID
RAID5	3	optional	yes	Size of the smallest partition multiplied by (number of devices in RAID minus 1)
RAID6	4	optional	yes	Size of the smallest partition multiplied by (number of devices in RAID minus 2)
RAID10	2	optional	yes	Total of all partitions divided by the number of chunk copies (defaults to 2)

If you want to know more about Software RAID, have a look at *Software RAID HOWTO*[4].

To create an MD device, you need to have the desired partitions it should consist of marked for use in a RAID. (This is done in **partman** in the Partition settings menu where you should select Use as: → physical volume for RAID.)

---

[4] *http://www.tldp.org/HOWTO/Software-RAID-HOWTO.html*

Installation Guide

> **Note**
>
> Make sure that the system can be booted with the partitioning scheme you are planning. In general it will be necessary to create a separate file system for /boot when using RAID for the root (/) file system. Most boot loaders (including lilo and grub) do support mirrored (not striped!) RAID1, so using for example RAID5 for / and RAID1 for /boot can be an option.

> **Warning**
>
> Support for MD is a relatively new addition to the installer. You may experience problems for some RAID levels and in combination with some bootloaders if you try to use MD for the root (/) file system. For experienced users, it may be possible to work around some of these problems by executing some configuration or installation steps manually from a shell.

Next, you should choose Configure software RAID from the main **partman** menu. (The menu will only appear after you mark at least one partition for use as physical volume for RAID.) On the first screen of **mdcfg** simply select Create MD device. You will be presented with a list of supported types of MD devices, from which you should choose one (e.g. RAID1). What follows depends on the type of MD you selected.

- RAID0 is simple — you will be issued with the list of available RAID partitions and your only task is to select the partitions which will form the MD.
- RAID1 is a bit more tricky. First, you will be asked to enter the number of active devices and the number of spare devices which will form the MD. Next, you need to select from the list of available RAID partitions those that will be active and then those that will be spare. The count of selected partitions must be equal to the number provided earlier. Don't worry. If you make a mistake and select a different number of partitions, `debian-installer` won't let you continue until you correct the issue.
- RAID5 has a setup procedure similar to RAID1 with the exception that you need to use at least *three* active partitions.
- RAID6 also has a setup procedure similar to RAID1 except that at least *four* active partitions are required.
- RAID10 again has a setup procedure similar to RAID1 except in expert mode. In expert mode, `debian-installer` will ask you for the layout. The layout has two parts. The first part is the layout type. It is either n (for near copies), f (for far copies), or o (for offset copies). The second part is the number of copies to make of the data. There must be at least that many active devices so that all of the copies can be distributed onto different disks.

It is perfectly possible to have several types of MD at once. For example, if you have three 200 GB hard drives dedicated to MD, each containing two 100 GB partitions, you can combine the first partitions on all three disks into the RAID0 (fast 300 GB video editing partition) and use the other three partitions (2 active and 1 spare) for RAID1 (quite reliable 100 GB partition for /home).

After you set up MD devices to your liking, you can Finish **mdcfg** to return back to the **partman** to create filesystems on your new MD devices and assign them the usual attributes like mountpoints.

6.3.2.4. Configuring the Logical Volume Manager (LVM)

If you are working with computers at the level of system administrator or "advanced" user, you have surely seen the situation where some disk partition (usually the most important one) was short on space, while some other partition was grossly underused and you had to manage this situation by moving stuff around, symlinking, etc.

To avoid the described situation you can use Logical Volume Manager (LVM). Simply said, with LVM you can combine your partitions (*physical volumes* in LVM lingo) to form a virtual disk (so called *volume group*), which can then be divided into virtual partitions (*logical volumes*). The point is that logical volumes (and of course underlying volume groups) can span across several physical disks.

Now when you realize you need more space for your old 160GB /home partition, you can simply add a new 300GB disk to the computer, join it with your existing volume group and then resize the logical volume which holds your /home filesystem and voila — your users have some room again on their renewed 460GB partition. This example is of course a bit oversimplified. If you haven't read it yet, you should consult the *LVM HOWTO*[5].

LVM setup in debian-installer is quite simple and completely supported inside **partman**. First, you have to mark the partition(s) to be used as physical volumes for LVM. This is done in the Partition settings menu where you should select Use as: → physical volume for LVM.

When you return to the main **partman** screen, you will see a new option Configure the Logical Volume Manager. When you select that, you will first be asked to confirm pending changes to the partition table (if any) and after that the LVM configuration menu will be shown. Above the menu a summary of the LVM configuration is shown. The menu itself is context sensitive and only shows valid actions. The possible actions are:

- Display configuration details: shows LVM device structure, names and sizes of logical volumes and more

---

[5] *http://www.tldp.org/HOWTO/LVM-HOWTO.html*

Installation Guide

- Create volume group
- Create logical volume
- Delete volume group
- Delete logical volume
- Extend volume group
- Reduce volume group
- Finish: return to the main **partman** screen

Use the options in that menu to first create a volume group and then create your logical volumes inside it.

After you return to the main **partman** screen, any created logical volumes will be displayed in the same way as ordinary partitions (and you should treat them as such).

6.3.2.5. Configuring Encrypted Volumes

`debian-installer` allows you to set up encrypted partitions. Every file you write to such a partition is immediately saved to the device in encrypted form. Access to the encrypted data is granted only after entering the *passphrase* used when the encrypted partition was originally created. This feature is useful to protect sensitive data in case your laptop or hard drive gets stolen. The thief might get physical access to the hard drive, but without knowing the right passphrase, the data on the hard drive will look like random characters.

The two most important partitions to encrypt are: the home partition, where your private data resides, and the swap partition, where sensitive data might be stored temporarily during operation. Of course, nothing prevents you from encrypting any other partitions that might be of interest. For example /var where database servers, mail servers or print servers store their data, or /tmp which is used by various programs to store potentially interesting temporary files. Some people may even want to encrypt their whole system. The only exception is the /boot partition which must remain unencrypted, because currently there is no way to load the kernel from an encrypted partition.

> **Note**
>
> Please note that the performance of encrypted partitions will be less than that of unencrypted ones because the data needs to be decrypted or encrypted for every read or write. The performance impact depends on your CPU speed, chosen cipher and a key length.

To use encryption, you have to create a new partition by selecting some free space in the main partitioning menu. Another option is to choose an existing partition (e.g. a regular partition, an LVM logical volume or a RAID volume). In the Partition settings menu, you

Ubuntu 9.10

need to select physical volume for encryption at the Use as: option. The menu will then change to include several cryptographic options for the partition.

debian-installer supports several encryption methods. The default method is *dm-crypt* (included in newer Linux kernels, able to host LVM physical volumes), the other is *loop-AES* (older, maintained separately from the Linux kernel tree). Unless you have compelling reasons to do otherwise, it is recommended to use the default.

First, let's have a look at the options available when you select **Device-mapper (dm-crypt)** as the encryption method. As always: when in doubt, use the defaults, because they have been carefully chosen with security in mind.

Encryption: aes

This option lets you select the encryption algorithm (*cipher*) which will be used to encrypt the data on the partition. debian-installer currently supports the following block ciphers: *aes*, *blowfish*, *serpent*, and *twofish*. It is beyond the scope of this document to discuss the qualities of these different algorithms, however, it might help your decision to know that in 2000, *AES* was chosen by the American National Institute of Standards and Technology as the standard encryption algorithm for protecting sensitive information in the 21st century.

Key size: 256

Here you can specify the length of the encryption key. With a larger key size, the strength of the encryption is generally improved. On the other hand, increasing the length of the key usually has a negative impact on performance. Available key sizes vary depending on the cipher.

IV algorithm: cbc-essiv:sha256

The *Initialization Vector* or *IV* algorithm is used in cryptography to ensure that applying the cipher on the same *clear text* data with the same key always produces a unique *cipher text*. The idea is to prevent the attacker from deducing information from repeated patterns in the encrypted data.

From the provided alternatives, the default **cbc-essiv:sha256** is currently the least vulnerable to known attacks. Use the other alternatives only when you need to ensure compatibility with some previously installed system that is not able to use newer algorithms.

Encryption key: Passphrase

Here you can choose the type of the encryption key for this partition.

Installation Guide

Passphrase

> The encryption key will be computed[6] on the basis of a passphrase which you will be able to enter later in the process.

Random key

> A new encryption key will be generated from random data each time you try to bring up the encrypted partition. In other words: on every shutdown the content of the partition will be lost as the key is deleted from memory. (Of course, you could try to guess the key with a brute force attack, but unless there is an unknown weakness in the cipher algorithm, it is not achievable in our lifetime.)

> Random keys are useful for swap partitions because you do not need to bother yourself with remembering the passphrase or wiping sensitive information from the swap partition before shutting down your computer. However, it also means that you will *not* be able to use the "suspend-to-disk" functionality offered by newer Linux kernels as it will be impossible (during a subsequent boot) to recover the suspended data written to the swap partition.

Erase data: `yes`

> Determines whether the content of this partition should be overwritten with random data before setting up the encryption. This is recommended because it might otherwise be possible for an attacker to discern which parts of the partition are in use and which are not. In addition, this will make it harder to recover any leftover data from previous installations[7].

If you select Encryption method: → Loopback (loop-AES), the menu changes to provide the following options:

Encryption: `AES256`

> For loop-AES, unlike dm-crypt, the options for cipher and key size are combined, so you can select both at the same time. Please see the above sections on ciphers and key sizes for further information.

Encryption key: `Keyfile (GnuPG)`

> Here you can select the type of the encryption key for this partition.

---

[6] Using a passphrase as the key currently means that the partition will be set up using *LUKS* (http://luks.endorphin.org/).
[7] It is believed that the guys from three-letter agencies can restore the data even after several rewrites of the magnetooptical media, though.

Ubuntu 9.10

Keyfile (GnuPG)

The encryption key will be generated from random data during the installation. Moreover this key will be encrypted with **GnuPG**, so to use it, you will need to enter the proper passphrase (you will be asked to provide one later in the process).

Random key

Please see the section on random keys above.

Erase data: `yes`

Please see the the section on erasing data above.

After you have selected the desired parameters for your encrypted partitions, return back to the main partitioning menu. There should now be a new menu item called Configure encrypted volumes. After you select it, you will be asked to confirm the deletion of data on partitions marked to be erased and possibly other actions such as writing a new partition table. For large partitions this might take some time.

Next you will be asked to enter a passphrase for partitions configured to use one. Good passphrases should be longer than 8 characters, should be a mixture of letters, numbers and other characters and should not contain common dictionary words or information easily associable with you (such as birthdates, hobbies, pet names, names of family members or relatives, etc.).

> ⚠️ **Warning**
>
> Before you input any passphrases, you should have made sure that your keyboard is configured correctly and generates the expected characters. If you are unsure, you can switch to the second virtual console and type some text at the prompt. This ensures that you won't be surprised later, e.g. by trying to input a passphrase using a qwerty keyboard layout when you used an azerty layout during the installation. This situation can have several causes. Maybe you switched to another keyboard layout during the installation, or the selected keyboard layout might not have been set up yet when entering the passphrase for the root file system.

If you selected to use methods other than a passphrase to create encryption keys, they will be generated now. Because the kernel may not have gathered a sufficient amount of entropy at this early stage of the installation, the process may take a long time. You can help speed up the process by generating entropy: e.g. by pressing random keys, or by switching to the shell on the second virtual console and generating some network and disk traffic (downloading some files, feeding big files into `/dev/null`, etc.). This will be repeated for each partition to be encrypted.

Installation Guide

After returning to the main partitioning menu, you will see all encrypted volumes as additional partitions which can be configured in the same way as ordinary partitions. The following example shows two different volumes. The first one is encrypted via dm-crypt, the second one via loop-AES.

```
Encrypted volume (sda2_crypt) - 115.1 GB Linux device-mapper
     #1 115.1 GB   F ext3

Loopback (loop0) - 515.2 MB AES256 keyfile
     #1 515.2 MB   F ext3
```

Now is the time to assign mount points to the volumes and optionally change the file system types if the defaults do not suit you.

Pay attention to the identifiers in parentheses (`sda2_crypt` and `loop0` in this case) and the mount points you assigned to each encrypted volume. You will need this information later when booting the new system. The differences between the ordinary boot process and the boot process with encryption involved will be covered later in *the section called "Mounting encrypted volumes"*.

Once you are satisfied with the partitioning scheme, continue with the installation.

6.3.3. Installing the Base System

Although this stage is the least problematic, it consumes a significant fraction of the install because it downloads, verifies and unpacks the whole base system. If you have a slow computer or network connection, this could take some time.

During installation of the base system, package unpacking and setup messages are redirected to **tty4**. You can access this terminal by pressing **Left Alt+ F4**; get back to the main installer process with **Left Alt+ F1**.

The unpack/setup messages generated during this phase are also saved in `/var/log/syslog`. You can check them there if the installation is performed over a serial console.

As part of the installation, a Linux kernel will be installed. At the default priority, the installer will choose one for you that best matches your hardware. In lower priority modes, you will be able to choose from a list of available kernels.

6.3.4. Setting Up Users And Passwords

After the base system has been installed, the installer will allow you to set up the "root" account and/or an account for the first user. Other user accounts can be created after the installation has been completed.

6.3.4.1. Create an Ordinary User

The system will ask you whether you wish to create an ordinary user account at this point. This account should be your main personal log-in.

The account you create at this point will be given *root* privileges by means of the **sudo** command, and the root account itself will have login disabled. If you wish, you can enable the root account later by setting a password for it with the command `sudo passwd root`.

You should *not* use the root account for daily use or as your personal login, nor should you use **sudo** except when root privileges are really required.

Why not? Well, one reason to avoid using root's privileges is that it is very easy to do irreparable damage as root. Another reason is that you might be tricked into running a *Trojan-horse* program — that is a program that takes advantage of your super-user powers to compromise the security of your system behind your back. Any good book on Unix system administration will cover this topic in more detail — consider reading one if it is new to you.

You will first be prompted for the user's full name. Then you'll be asked for a name for the user account; generally your first name or something similar will suffice and indeed will be the default. Finally, you will be prompted for a password for this account.

If at any point after installation you would like to create another account, use the **adduser** command.

6.3.5. Installing Additional Software

At this point you have a usable but limited system. Most users will want to install additional software on the system to tune it to their needs, and the installer allows you do so. This step can take even longer than installing the base system if you have a slow computer or network connection.

6.3.5.1. Configuring apt

One of the tools used to install packages on a Debian GNU/Linux system is a program called **apt-get**, from the apt package[8]. Other front-ends for package management, like **aptitude** and **synaptic**, are also in use. These front-ends are recommended for new users,

---

[8] Note that the program which actually installs the packages is called **dpkg**. However, this program is more of a low-level tool. **apt-get** is a higher-level tool, which will invoke **dpkg** as appropriate. It knows how to retrieve packages from your CD, the network, or wherever. It is also able to automatically install other packages which are required to make the package you're trying to install work correctly.

Installation Guide

since they integrate some additional features (package searching and status checks) in a nice user interface. In fact, **aptitude** is now the recommended utility for package management.

apt must be configured so that it knows from where to retrieve packages. The results of this configuration are written to the file /etc/apt/sources.list. You can examine and edit this file to your liking after the installation is complete.

If you are installing at default priority, the installer will largely take care of the configuration automatically, based on the installation method you are using and possibly using choices made earlier in the installation. In most cases the installer will automatically add a security mirror and, if you are installing the stable distribution, a mirror for the "volatile" update service.

If you are installing at a lower priority (e.g. in expert mode), you will be able to make more decisions yourself. You can choose whether or not to use the security and/or volatile update services, and you can choose to add packages from the "contrib" and "non-free" sections of the archive.

6.3.5.1.1 Installing from more than one CD or DVD

If you are installing from a CD or a DVD that is part of a larger set, the installer will ask if you want to scan additional CDs or DVDs. If you have additional CDs or DVDs available, you probably want to do this so the installer can use the packages included on them.

If you do not have any additional CDs or DVDs, that is no problem: using them is not required. If you also do not use a network mirror (as explained in the next section), it can mean that not all packages belonging to the tasks you select in the next step of the installation can be installed.

> **Note**
>
> Packages are included on CDs (and DVDs) in the order of their popularity. This means that for most uses only the first CDs in a set are needed and that only very few people actually use any of the packages included on the last CDs in a set.
>
> It also means that buying or downloading and burning a full CD set is just a waste of money as you'll never use most of them. In most cases you are better off getting only the first 3 to 8 CDs and installing any additional packages you may need from the Internet by using a mirror. The same goes for DVD sets: the first DVD, or maybe the first two DVDs will cover most needs.
>
> A good rule of thumb is that for a regular desktop installation (using the GNOME desktop environment) only the first three CDs are needed. For the alternative desktop environments (KDE or Xfce), additional CDs are needed. The first DVD easily covers all three desktop environments.

Ubuntu 9.10

If you do scan multiple CDs or DVDs, the installer will prompt you to exchange them when it needs packages from another CD/DVD than the one currently in the drive. Note that only CDs or DVDs that belong to the same set should be scanned. The order in which they are scanned does not really matter, but scanning them in ascending order will reduce the chance of mistakes.

6.3.5.1.2 Using a network mirror

One question that will be asked during most installs is whether or not to use a network mirror as a source for packages. In most cases the default answer should be fine, but there are some exceptions.

If you are *not* installing from a full CD or DVD or using a full CD/DVD image, you really should use a network mirror as otherwise you will end up with only a very minimal system. However, if you have a limited Internet connection it is best *not* to select the `desktop` task in the next step of the installation.

If you are installing from a single full CD or using a full CD image, using a network mirror is not required, but is still strongly recommended because a single CD contains only a fairly limited number of packages. If you have a limited Internet connection it may still be best to *not* select a network mirror here, but to finish the installation using only what's available on the CD and selectively install additional packages after the installation (i.e. after you have rebooted into the new system).

If you are installing from a DVD or using a DVD image, any packages needed during the installation should be present on the first DVD. The same is true if you have scanned multiple CDs as explained in the previous section. Use of a network mirror is optional.

One advantage of adding a network mirror is that updates that have occurred since the CD/DVD set was created and have been included in a point release, will become available for installation, thus extending the life of your CD/DVD set without compromising the security or stability of the installed system.

In summary: selecting a network mirror is generally a good idea, except if you do not have a good Internet connection. If the current version of a package is available from CD/DVD, the installer will always use that. The amount of data that will be downloaded if you do select a mirror thus depends on

1. the tasks you select in the next step of the installation,
2. which packages are needed for those tasks,
3. which of those packages are present on the CDs or DVDs you have scanned, and
4. whether any updated versions of packages included on the CDs or DVDs are available from a mirror (either a regular package mirror, or a mirror for security or volatile updates).

Installation Guide

Note that the last point means that, even if you choose not to use a network mirror, some packages may still be downloaded from the Internet if there is a security or volatile update available for them and those services have been configured.

6.3.5.2. Selecting and Installing Software

During the installation process, you may be given the opportunity to select additional software to install. Rather than picking individual software packages from the 22600 available packages, this stage of the installation process focuses on selecting and installing predefined collections of software to quickly set up your computer to perform various tasks.

(If you are installing from a full Ubuntu CD, rather than from the server CD or by booting the installer over the network, then this stage of the installation process will simply automatically install the set of packages that make up the Ubuntu desktop, and you can ignore the rest of this section.)

So, you have the ability to choose *tasks* first, and then add on more individual packages later. These tasks loosely represent a number of different jobs or things you want to do with your computer, such as "Desktop environment", "Web server", or "Print server"[9]. *the section called "Disk Space Needed for Tasks"* lists the space requirements for the available tasks.

Some tasks may be pre-selected based on the characteristics of the computer you are installing. If you disagree with these selections you can deselect them. You can even opt to install no tasks at all at this point.

> **Note**
>
> Unless you are using the special KDE or Xfce CDs, the "Desktop environment" task will install the GNOME desktop environment.
>
> It is not possible to interactively select a different desktop during the installation. However, it *is* possible to get debian-installer to install a KDE desktop environment instead of GNOME by using preseeding (see *the section called "Package selection"*) or by adding the parameter desktop=kde at the boot prompt when starting the installer. Alternatively the more lightweight Xfce desktop environment can be selected by using desktop=xfce.
>
> Note that this will only work if the packages needed for KDE or Xfce are actually available. If you are installing using a single full CD image, they will need to be

---

[9] You should know that to present this list, the installer is merely invoking the **tasksel** program. It can be run at any time after installation to install more packages (or remove them), or you can use a more fine-grained tool such as **aptitude**. If you are looking for a specific single package, after installation is complete, simply run `aptitude install package`, where `package` is the name of the package you are looking for.

> downloaded from a mirror as most needed packages are only included on later CDs; installing KDE or Xfce this way should work fine if you are using a DVD image or any other installation method.
>
> The various server tasks will install software roughly as follows. DNS server: `bind9`; File server: `samba`, `nfs`; Mail server: `exim4`, `spamassassin`, `uw-imap`; Print server: `cups`; SQL database: `postgresql`; Web server: `apache2`.

Once you've selected your tasks, select **Continue**. At this point, **aptitude** will install the packages that are part of the selected tasks. If a particular program needs more information from the user, it will prompt you during this process.

> **Note**
>
> In the standard user interface of the installer, you can use the space bar to toggle selection of a task.

You should be aware that especially the Desktop task is very large. Especially when installing from a normal CD-ROM in combination with a mirror for packages not on the CD-ROM, the installer may want to retrieve a lot of packages over the network. If you have a relatively slow Internet connection, this can take a long time. There is no option to cancel the installation of packages once it has started.

Even when packages are included on the CD-ROM, the installer may still retrieve them from the mirror if the version available on the mirror is more recent than the one included on the CD-ROM. If you are installing the stable distribution, this can happen after a point release (an update of the original stable release); if you are installing the testing distribution this will happen if you are using an older image.

6.3.6. Making Your System Bootable

If you are installing a diskless workstation, obviously, booting off the local disk isn't a meaningful option, and this step will be skipped.

6.3.6.1. Detecting other operating systems

Before a boot loader is installed, the installer will attempt to probe for other operating systems which are installed on the machine. If it finds a supported operating system, you will be informed of this during the boot loader installation step, and the computer will be configured to boot this other operating system in addition to Ubuntu.

Note that multiple operating systems booting on a single machine is still something of a black art. The automatic support for detecting and setting up boot loaders to boot other operating systems varies by architecture and even by subarchitecture. If it does not work you should consult your boot manager's documentation for more information.

Installation Guide

6.3.6.2. Install the Grub Boot Loader on a Hard Disk

The main i386 boot loader is called "grub". Grub is a flexible and robust boot loader and a good default choice for new users and old hands alike.

By default, grub will be installed into the Master Boot Record (MBR), where it will take over complete control of the boot process. If you prefer, you can install it elsewhere. See the grub manual for complete information.

If you do not want to install grub, use the **Go Back** button to get to the main menu, and from there select whatever bootloader you would like to use.

6.3.6.3. Install the LILO Boot Loader on a Hard Disk

The second i386 boot loader is called "LILO". It is an old complex program which offers lots of functionality, including DOS, Windows, and OS/2 boot management. Please carefully read the instructions in the directory `/usr/share/doc/lilo/` if you have special needs; also see the *LILO mini-HOWTO*[10].

> **Note**
>
> Currently the LILO installation will only create menu entries for other operating systems if these can be *chainloaded*. This means you may have to manually add a menu entry for operating systems like GNU/Linux and GNU/Hurd after the installation.

`debian-installer` offers you three choices on where to install the **LILO** boot loader:

Master Boot Record (MBR)

> This way the **LILO** will take complete control of the boot process.

new Ubuntu partition

> Choose this if you want to use another boot manager. **LILO** will install itself at the beginning of the new Ubuntu partition and it will serve as a secondary boot loader.

Other choice

> Useful for advanced users who want to install **LILO** somewhere else. In this case you will be asked for desired location. You can use traditional device names such as `/dev/hda` or `/dev/sda`.

If you can no longer boot into Windows 9x (or DOS) after this step, you'll need to use a Windows 9x (MS-DOS) boot disk and use the `fdisk /mbr` command to reinstall the MS-

---

[10] *http://www.tldp.org/HOWTO/LILO.html*

Ubuntu 9.10

DOS master boot record — however, this means that you'll need to use some other way to get back into Ubuntu!

6.3.6.4. Continue Without Boot Loader

This option can be used to complete the installation even when no boot loader is to be installed, either because the arch/subarch doesn't provide one, or because none is desired (e.g. you will use existing boot loader).

If you plan to manually configure your bootloader, you should check the name of the installed kernel in `/target/boot`. You should also check that directory for the presence of an *initrd*; if one is present, you will probably have to instruct your bootloader to use it. Other information you will need are the disk and partition you selected for your / filesystem and, if you chose to install `/boot` on a separate partition, also your `/boot` filesystem.

6.3.7. Finishing the Installation

This is the last step in the Debian installation process during which the installer will do any last minute tasks. It mostly consists of tidying up after the `debian-installer`.

6.3.7.1. Setting the System Clock

The installer may ask you if the computer's clock is set to UTC. Normally this question is avoided if possible and the installer tries to work out whether the clock is set to UTC based on things like what other operating systems are installed.

In expert mode you will always be able to choose whether or not the clock is set to UTC. Systems that (also) run Dos or Windows are normally set to local time. If you want to dual-boot, select local time instead of UTC.

At this point `debian-installer` will also attempt to save the current time to the system's hardware clock. This will be done either in UTC or local time, depending on the selection that was just made.

6.3.7.2. Reboot the System

You will be prompted to remove the boot media (CD, floppy, etc) that you used to boot the installer. After that the system will be rebooted into your new Ubuntu system.

6.3.8. Miscellaneous

The components listed in this section are usually not involved in the installation process, but are waiting in the background to help the user in case something goes wrong.

Installation Guide

6.3.8.1. Saving the installation logs

If the installation is successful, the logfiles created during the installation process will be automatically saved to `/var/log/installer/` on your new Ubuntu system.

Choosing Save debug logs from the main menu allows you to save the log files to a floppy disk, network, hard disk, or other media. This can be useful if you encounter fatal problems during the installation and wish to study the logs on another system or attach them to an installation report.

6.3.8.2. Using the Shell and Viewing the Logs

There are several methods you can use to get a shell while running an installation. On most systems, and if you are not installing over serial console, the easiest method is to switch to the second *virtual console* by pressing **Left Alt**+ **F2**[11] (on a Mac keyboard, **Option**+ **F2**). Use **Left Alt**+ **F1** to switch back to the installer itself.

For the graphical installer see also *the section called "Using the graphical installer"*.

If you cannot switch consoles, there is also an Execute a Shell item on the main menu that can be used to start a shell. You can get to the main menu from most dialogs by using the **Go Back** button one or more times. Type `exit` to close the shell and return to the installer.

At this point you are booted from the RAM disk, and there is a limited set of Unix utilities available for your use. You can see what programs are available with the command **ls /bin /sbin /usr/bin /usr/sbin** and by typing **help**. The shell is a Bourne shell clone called **ash** and has some nice features like autocompletion and history.

To edit and view files, use the text editor **nano**. Log files for the installation system can be found in the `/var/log` directory.

> **Note**
>
> Although you can do basically anything in a shell that the available commands allow you to do, the option to use a shell is really only there in case something goes wrong and for debugging.
>
> Doing things manually from the shell may interfere with the installation process and result in errors or an incomplete installation. In particular, you should always use let the installer activate your swap partition and not do this yourself from a shell.

---

[11] That is: press the **Alt** key on the left-hand side of the **space bar** and the **F2** function key at the same time.

6.3.8.3. Installation Over the Network

One of the more interesting components is *network-console*. It allows you to do a large part of the installation over the network via SSH. The use of the network implies you will have to perform the first steps of the installation from the console, at least to the point of setting up the networking. (Although you can automate that part with *the section called "Automatic Installation"*.)

This component is not loaded into the main installation menu by default, so you have to explicitly ask for it. If you are installing from CD, you need to boot with medium priority or otherwise invoke the main installation menu and choose Load installer components from CD and from the list of additional components select network-console: Continue installation remotely using SSH. Successful load is indicated by a new menu entry called Continue installation remotely using SSH.

After selecting this new entry, you will be asked for a new password to be used for connecting to the installation system and for its confirmation. That's all. Now you should see a screen which instructs you to login remotely as the user *installer* with the password you just provided. Another important detail to notice on this screen is the fingerprint of this system. You need to transfer the fingerprint securely to the "person who will continue the installation remotely".

Should you decide to continue with the installation locally, you can always press **Enter**, which will bring you back to the main menu, where you can select another component.

Now let's switch to the other side of the wire. As a prerequisite, you need to configure your terminal for UTF-8 encoding, because that is what the installation system uses. If you do not, remote installation will be still possible, but you may encounter strange display artefacts like destroyed dialog borders or unreadable non-ascii characters. Establishing a connection with the installation system is as simple as typing:

```
$ ssh -l installer install_host
```

Where `install_host` is either the name or IP address of the computer being installed. Before the actual login the fingerprint of the remote system will be displayed and you will have to confirm that it is correct.

> **Note**
>
> The **ssh** server in the installer uses a default configuration that does not send keep-alive packets. In principle, a connection to the system being installed should be kept open indefinitely. However, in some situations — depending on your local network setup — the connection may be lost after some period of inactivity. One common case where this can happen is when there is some form of Network Address

Translation (NAT) somewhere between the client and the system being installed. Depending on at which point of the installation the connection was lost, you may or may not be able to resume the installation after reconnecting.

You may be able to avoid the connection being dropped by adding the option `-o ServerAliveInterval=` *value* when starting the **ssh** connection, or by adding that option in your **ssh** configuration file. Note however that in some cases adding this option may also *cause* a connection to be dropped (for example if keep-alive packets are sent during a brief network outage, from which **ssh** would otherwise have recovered), so it should only be used when needed.

> **Note**
>
> If you install several computers in turn and they happen to have the same IP address or hostname, **ssh** will refuse to connect to such host. The reason is that it will have different fingerprint, which is usually a sign of a spoofing attack. If you are sure this is not the case, you will need to delete the relevant line from ~/.ssh/known_hosts[12] and try again.

After the login you will be presented with an initial screen where you have two possibilities called Start menu and Start shell. The former brings you to the main installer menu, where you can continue with the installation as usual. The latter starts a shell from which you can examine and possibly fix the remote system. You should only start one SSH session for the installation menu, but may start multiple sessions for shells.

> **Warning**
>
> After you have started the installation remotely over SSH, you should not go back to the installation session running on the local console. Doing so may corrupt the database that holds the configuration of the new system. This in turn may result in a failed installation or problems with the installed system.

6.4. Loading Missing Firmware

As described in *the section called "Devices Requiring Firmware"*, some devices require firmware to be loaded. In most cases the device will not work at all if the firmware is not available; sometimes basic functionality is not impaired if it is missing and the firmware is only needed to enable additional features.

If a device driver requests firmware that is not available, `debian-installer` will display a dialog offering to load the missing firmware. If this option is selected, `debian-installer`

---

[12] The following command will remove an existing entry for a host: **ssh-keygen -R <***hostname* | *IP address***>**.

will scan available devices for either loose firmware files or packages containing firmware.
If found, the firmware will be copied to the correct location (/lib/firmware) and the driver
module will be reloaded.

> **Note**
>
> Which devices are scanned and which file systems are supported depends on the
> architecture, the installation method and the stage of the installation. Especially
> during the early stages of the installation, loading the firmware is most likely to
> succeed from a FAT-formatted floppy disk or USB stick. On i386 and amd64
> firmware can also be loaded from an MMC or SD card.

Note that it is possible to skip loading the firmware if you know the device will also
function without it, or if the device is not needed during the installation.

> **Warning**
>
> Support for loading firmware is still relatively basic and is likely to be improved in
> future releases of the installer. Currently debian-installer will for example not
> display any warning if you choose to load missing firmware, but the requested
> firmware is not found. Please report any issues you encounter by filing an
> installation report (see *the section called "Submitting Installation Reports"*).

6.4.1. Preparing a medium

Although in some cases the firmware can also be loaded from a partition on a hard disk, the
most common method to load firmware will be from some removable medium such as a
floppy disk or a USB stick. The firmware files or packages must be placed in either the root
directory or a directory named /firmware of the file system on the medium. The
recommended file system to use is FAT as that is most certain to be supported during the
early stages of the installation.

Tarballs containing current packages for the most common firmware are available from:

- *http://cdimage.debian.org/cdimage/unofficial/non-free/firmware/*

Just download the tarball for the correct release and unpack it to the file system on the
medium.

If the firmware you need is not included in the tarball, you can also download specific
firmware packages from the (non-free section of the) archive. The following overview
should list most available firmware packages but is not guaranteed to be complete and may
also contain non-firmware packages:

- *http://packages.debian.org/search?keywords=firmware*

It is also possible to copy individual firmware files to the medium. Loose firmware could be obtained for example from an already installed system or from a hardware vendor.

6.4.2. Firmware and the Installed System

Any firmware loaded during the installation will be copied automatically to the installed system. In most cases this will ensure that the device that requires the firmware will also work correctly after the system is rebooted into the installed system. However, if the installed system runs a different kernel version from the installer there is a slight chance that the firmware cannot be loaded due to version skew.

If the firmware was loaded from a firmware package, `debian-installer` will also install this package for the installed system and will automatically add the non-free section of the package archive in APT's `sources.list`. This has the advantage that the firmware should be updated automatically if a new version becomes available.

If loading the firmware was skipped during the installation, the relevant device will probably not work with the installed system until the firmware (package) is installed manually.

> **Note**
>
> If the firmware was loaded from loose firmware files, the firmware copied to the installed system will *not* be automatically updated unless the corresponding firmware package (if available) is installed after the installation is completed.

Chapter 7. Booting Into Your New Ubuntu System

7.1. The Moment of Truth

Your system's first boot on its own power is what electrical engineers call the "smoke test".

If you did a default installation, the first thing you should see when you boot the system is the menu of the grub or possibly the lilo bootloader. The first choices in the menu will be for your new Ubuntu system. If you had any other operating systems on your computer (like Windows) that were detected by the installation system, those will be listed lower down in the menu.

If the system fails to start up correctly, don't panic. If the installation was successful, chances are good that there is only a relatively minor problem that is preventing the system from booting Ubuntu. In most cases such problems can be fixed without having to repeat the installation. One available option to fix boot problems is to use the installer's built-in rescue mode (see *the section called "Recovering a Broken System"*).

If you had any other operating systems on your computer that were not detected or not detected correctly, please file an installation report.

7.2. Mounting encrypted volumes

If you created encrypted volumes during the installation and assigned them mount points, you will be asked to enter the passphrase for each of these volumes during the boot. The actual procedure differs slightly between dm-crypt and loop-AES.

7.2.1. dm-crypt

For partitions encrypted using dm-crypt you will be shown the following prompt during the boot:

```
Starting early crypto disks... part_crypt(starting)
Enter LUKS passphrase:
```

In the first line of the prompt, *part* is the name of the underlying partition, e.g. sda2 or md0. You are now probably wondering *for which volume* you are actually entering the passphrase. Does it relate to your /home? Or to /var? Of course, if you have just one encrypted volume,

Installation Guide

this is easy and you can just enter the passphrase you used when setting up this volume. If you set up more than one encrypted volume during the installation, the notes you wrote down as the last step in *the section called "Configuring Encrypted Volumes"* come in handy. If you did not make a note of the mapping between `part_crypt` and the mount points before, you can still find it in `/etc/crypttab` and `/etc/fstab` of your new system.

The prompt may look somewhat different when an encrypted root file system is mounted. This depends on which initramfs generator was used to generate the initrd used to boot the system. The example below is for an initrd generated using `initramfs-tools`:

```
Begin: Mounting

root file system... ...
Begin: Running /scripts/local-top ...
Enter LUKS passphrase:
```

No characters (even asterisks) will be shown while entering the passphrase. If you enter the wrong passphrase, you have two more tries to correct it. After the third try the boot process will skip this volume and continue to mount the next filesystem. Please see *the section called "Troubleshooting"* for further information.

After entering all passphrases the boot should continue as usual.

7.2.2. loop-AES

For partitions encrypted using loop-AES you will be shown the following prompt during the boot:

```
Checking loop-encrypted file systems.
Setting up /dev/loopX (/mountpoint)
Password:
```

No characters (even asterisks) will be shown while entering the passphrase. If you enter the wrong passphrase, you have two more tries to correct it. After the third try the boot process will skip this volume and continue to mount the next filesystem. Please see *the section called "Troubleshooting"* for further information.

After entering all passphrases the boot should continue as usual.

7.2.3. Troubleshooting

If some of the encrypted volumes could not be mounted because a wrong passphrase was entered, you will have to mount them manually after the boot. There are several cases.

- The first case concerns the root partition. When it is not mounted correctly, the boot process will halt and you will have to reboot the computer to try again.

Ubuntu 9.10

- The easiest case is for encrypted volumes holding data like /home or /srv. You can simply mount them manually after the boot. For loop-AES this is a one-step operation:

    ```
    # mount /mount_point
    Password:
    ```

    where /mount_point should be replaced by the particular directory (e.g. /home). The only difference from an ordinary mount is that you will be asked to enter the passphrase for this volume.

    For dm-crypt this is a bit trickier. First you need to register the volumes with **device mapper** by running:

    ```
    # /etc/init.d/cryptdisks start
    ```

    This will scan all volumes mentioned in /etc/crypttab and will create appropriate devices under the /dev directory after entering the correct passphrases. (Already registered volumes will be skipped, so you can repeat this command several times without worrying.) After successful registration you can simply mount the volumes the usual way:

    ```
    # mount /mount_point
    ```

- If any volume holding noncritical system files could not be mounted (/usr or /var), the system should still boot and you should be able to mount the volumes manually like in the previous case. However, you will also need to (re)start any services usually running in your default runlevel because it is very likely that they were not started. The easiest way to achieve this is by switching to the first runlevel and back by entering

    ```
    # init 1
    ```

    at the shell prompt and pressing **Control+ D** when asked for the root password.

7.3. Log In

Once your system boots, you'll be presented with the login prompt. Log in using the personal login and password you selected during the installation process. Your system is now ready for use.

If you are a new user, you may want to explore the documentation which is already installed on your system as you start to use it. There are currently several documentation systems, work is proceeding on integrating the different types of documentation. Here are a few starting points.

Documentation accompanying programs you have installed can be found in /usr/share/doc/, under a subdirectory named after the program (or, more precise, the

Installation Guide

Debian package that contains the program). However, more extensive documentation is often packaged separately in special documentation packages that are mostly not installed by default. For example, documentation about the package management tool **apt** can be found in the packages `apt-doc` or `apt-howto`.

In addition, there are some special folders within the `/usr/share/doc/` hierarchy. Linux HOWTOs are installed in *.gz* (compressed) format, in `/usr/share/doc/HOWTO/en-txt/`. After installing `dhelp`, you will find a browsable index of documentation in `/usr/share/doc/HTML/index.html`.

One easy way to view these documents using a text based browser is to enter the following commands:

```
$ cd /usr/share/doc/
$ w3m .
```

The dot after the **w3m** command tells it to show the contents of the current directory.

If you have a graphical desktop environment installed, you can also use its web browser. Start the web browser from the application menu and enter **/usr/share/doc/** in the address bar.

You can also type **info** *command* or **man** *command* to see documentation on most commands available at the command prompt. Typing **help** will display help on shell commands. And typing a command followed by **--help** will usually display a short summary of the command's usage. If a command's results scroll past the top of the screen, type | **more** after the command to cause the results to pause before scrolling past the top of the screen. To see a list of all commands available which begin with a certain letter, type the letter and then two tabs.

Chapter 8.
Next Steps and Where to Go From Here

8.1. Shutting down the system

To shut down a running Linux system, you must not reboot with the reset switch on the front or back of your computer, or just turn off the computer. Linux should be shut down in a controlled manner, otherwise files might get lost and/or disk damage might occur. If you run a desktop environment, there is usually an option to "log out" available from the application menu that allows you to shutdown (or reboot) the system.

Alternatively you can press the key combination **Ctrl+ Alt+ Del** . A last option is to log in as root and type one of the commands **poweroff**, **halt** or **shutdown -h now** if either of the key combinations do not work or you prefer to type commands; use **reboot** to reboot the system.

8.2. If You Are New to Unix

If you are new to Unix, you probably should go out and buy some books and do some reading. A lot of valuable information can also be found in the *Debian Reference*[1]. This *list of Unix FAQs*[2] contains a number of UseNet documents which provide a nice historical reference.

Linux is an implementation of Unix. The *Linux Documentation Project (LDP)*[3] collects a number of HOWTOs and online books relating to Linux. Most of these documents can be installed locally; just install the `doc-linux-html` package (HTML versions) or the `doc-linux-text` package (ASCII versions), then look in `/usr/share/doc/HOWTO`. International versions of the LDP HOWTOs are also available as Ubuntu packages.

8.3. Orienting Yourself to Ubuntu

Ubuntu is a little different from other distributions. Even if you're familiar with Linux in other distributions, there are things you should know about Ubuntu to help you to keep

---

[1] *http://www.debian.org/doc/user-manuals#quick-reference*
[2] *http://www.faqs.org/faqs/unix-faq/*
[3] *http://www.tldp.org/*

your system in a good, clean state. This chapter contains material to help you get oriented; it is not intended to be a tutorial for how to use Ubuntu, but just a very brief glimpse of the system for the very rushed.

8.3.1. Ubuntu Packaging System

The most important concept to grasp is the Ubuntu packaging system, which may be familiar to those who have already used Debian GNU/Linux. In essence, large parts of your system should be considered under the control of the packaging system. These include:

- `/usr` (excluding `/usr/local`)
- `/var` (you could make `/var/local` and be safe in there)
- `/bin`
- `/sbin`
- `/lib`

For instance, if you replace `/usr/bin/perl`, that will work, but then if you upgrade your `perl` package, the file you put there will be replaced. Experts can get around this by putting packages on "hold" in **aptitude**.

One of the best installation methods is apt. You can use the command line version **apt-get**, the full-screen text version **aptitude**, or the graphical version **synaptic**. Note apt will also let you merge main, contrib, and non-free so you can have export-restricted packages as well as standard versions.

8.3.2. Application Version Management

Alternative versions of applications are managed by update-alternatives. If you are maintaining multiple versions of your applications, read the update-alternatives man page.

8.3.3. Cron Job Management

Any jobs under the purview of the system administrator should be in `/etc`, since they are configuration files. If you have a root cron job for daily, weekly, or monthly runs, put them in `/etc/cron.{daily,weekly,monthly}`. These are invoked from `/etc/crontab`, and will run in alphabetic order, which serializes them.

On the other hand, if you have a cron job that (a) needs to run as a special user, or (b) needs to run at a special time or frequency, you can use either `/etc/crontab`, or, better yet, `/etc/cron.d/whatever`. These particular files also have an extra field that allows you to stipulate the user account under which the cron job runs.

In either case, you just edit the files and cron will notice them automatically. There is no need to run a special command. For more information see cron(8), crontab(5), and `/usr/share/doc/cron/README.Debian`.

8.4. Further Reading and Information

If you need information about a particular program, you should first try `man program`, or `info program`.

There is lots of useful documentation in /usr/share/doc as well. In particular, /usr/share/doc/HOWTO and /usr/share/doc/FAQ contain lots of interesting information. To submit bugs, look at /usr/share/doc/debian/bug* . To read about Debian/Ubuntu-specific issues for particular programs, look at /usr/share/doc/(package name)/README.Debian.

The *Debian web site*[4] contains a large quantity of documentation about Debian. In particular, see the *Debian GNU/Linux FAQ*[5] and the *Debian Reference*[6]. An index of more Debian documentation is available from the *Debian Documentation Project*[7]. The Debian community is self-supporting; to subscribe to one or more of the Debian mailing lists, see the *Mail List Subscription*[8] page. Last, but not least, the *Debian Mailing List Archives*[9] contain a wealth of information on Debian.

Help on Ubuntu can be found on the *Ubuntu web site*[10]. In particular, see the *Ubuntu documentation*[11] pages for information on a wide variety of topics. The *Ubuntu mailing lists*[12] and the *Ubuntu Forums*[13] can be invaluable sources of help from the Ubuntu community.

A general source of information on GNU/Linux is the *Linux Documentation Project*[14]. There you will find the HOWTOs and pointers to other very valuable information on parts of a GNU/Linux system.

8.5. Setting Up Your System To Use E-Mail

Today, email is an important part of many people's life. As there are many options as to how to set it up, and as having it set up correctly is important for some Ubuntu utilities, we will try to cover the basics in this section.

---

[4] *http://www.debian.org/*

[5] *http://www.debian.org/doc/FAQ/*

[6] *http://www.debian.org/doc/user-manuals#quick-reference*

[7] *http://www.debian.org/doc/ddp*

[8] *http://www.debian.org/MailingLists/subscribe*

[9] *http://lists.debian.org/*

[10] *http://www.ubuntu.com/*

[11] *http://help.ubuntu.com/*

[12] *http://lists.ubuntu.com/*

[13] *http://www.ubuntuforums.org/*

[14] *http://www.tldp.org/*

There are three main functions that make up an e-mail system. First there is the *Mail User Agent* (MUA) which is the program a user actually uses to compose and read mails. Then there is the *Mail Transfer Agent* (MTA) that takes care of transferring messages from one computer to another. And last there is the *Mail Delivery Agent* (MDA) that takes care of delivering incoming mail to the user's inbox.

These three functions can be performed by separate programs, but they can also be combined in one or two programs. It is also possible to have different programs handle these functions for different types of mail.

On Linux and Unix systems **mutt** is historically a very popular MUA. Like most traditional Linux programs it is text based. It is often used in combination with **exim** or **sendmail** as MTA and **procmail** as MDA.

With the increasing popularity of graphical desktop systems, the use of graphical e-mail programs like GNOME's **evolution**, KDE's **kmail** or Mozilla's **thunderbird** is becoming more popular. These programs combine the function of a MUA, MTA and MDA, but can — and often are — also be used in combination with the traditional Linux tools.

8.5.1. Default E-Mail Configuration

Even if you are planning to use a graphical mail program, it is important that a traditional MTA/MDA is also installed and correctly set up on your Linux system. Reason is that various utilities running on the system[15] can send important notices by e-mail to inform the system administrator of (potential) problems or changes.

For this reason the packages `exim4` and `mutt` will be installed by default (provided you did not unselect the "standard" task during the installation). `exim4` is a combination MTA/MDA that is relatively small but very flexible. By default it will be configured to only handle e-mail local to the system itself and e-mails addressed to the system administrator (root account) will be delivered to the regular user account created during the installation[16].

When system e-mails are delivered they are added to a file in `/var/mail/account_name`. The e-mails can be read using **mutt**.

8.5.2. Sending E-Mails Outside The System

As mentioned earlier, the installed Ubuntu system is only set up to handle e-mail local to the system, not for sending mail to others nor for receiving mail from others.

---

[15] Examples are: **cron**, **quota**, **logcheck**, **aide**, …
[16] The forwarding of mail for root to the regular user account is configured in `/etc/aliases`. If no regular user account was created, the mail will of course be delivered to the root account itself.

Ubuntu 9.10

If you would like `exim4` to handle external e-mail, please refer to the next subsection for the basic available configuration options. Make sure to test that mail can be sent and received correctly.

If you intend to use a graphical mail program and use a mail server of your Internet Service Provider (ISP) or your company, there is not really any need to configure `exim4` for handling external e-mail. Just configure your favorite graphical mail program to use the correct servers to send and receive e-mail (how is outside the scope of this manual).

However, in that case you may need to configure individual utilities to correctly send e-mails. One such utility is **reportbug**, a program that facilitates submitting bug reports against Ubuntu packages. By default it expects to be able to use `exim4` to submit bug reports.

To correctly set up **reportbug** to use an external mail server, please run the command **reportbug --configure** and answer "no" to the question if an MTA is available. You will then be asked for the SMTP server to be used for submitting bug reports.

8.5.3. Configuring the Exim4 Mail Transport Agent

If you would like your system to also handle external e-mail, you will need to reconfigure the `exim4` package[17]:

```
# dpkg-reconfigure exim4-config
```

After entering that command (as root), you will be asked if you want split the configuration into small files. If you are unsure, select the default option.

Next you will be presented with several common mail scenarios. Choose the one that most closely resembles your needs.

internet site

Your system is connected to a network and your mail is sent and received directly using SMTP. On the following screens you will be asked a few basic questions, like your machine's mail name, or a list of domains for which you accept or relay mail.

mail sent by smarthost

In this scenario your outgoing mail is forwarded to another machine, called a "smarthost", which takes care of sending the message on to its destination. The smarthost also usually stores incoming mail addressed to your computer, so you don't need to be permanently online. That also means you have to download your mail from the smarthost via programs like fetchmail.

---

[17] You can of course also remove `exim4` and replace it with an alternative MTA/MDA.

In a lot of cases the smarthost will be your ISP's mail server, which makes this option very suitable for dial-up users. It can also be a company mail server, or even another system on your own network.

mail sent by smarthost; no local mail

This option is basically the same as the previous one except that the system will not be set up to handle mail for a local e-mail domain. Mail on the system itself (e.g. for the system administrator) will still be handled.

local delivery only

This is the option your system is configured for by default.

no configuration at this time

Choose this if you are absolutely convinced you know what you are doing. This will leave you with an unconfigured mail system — until you configure it, you won't be able to send or receive any mail and you may miss some important messages from your system utilities.

If none of these scenarios suits your needs, or if you need a finer grained setup, you will need to edit configuration files under the /etc/exim4 directory after the installation is complete. More information about exim4 may be found under /usr/share/doc/exim4; the file README.Debian.gz has further details about configuring exim4 and explains where to find additional documentation.

Note that sending mail directly to the Internet when you don't have an official domain name, can result in your mail being rejected because of anti-spam measures on receiving servers. Using your ISP's mail server is preferred. If you still do want to send out mail directly, you may want to use a different e-mail address than is generated by default. If you use exim4 as your MTA, this is possible by adding an entry in /etc/email-addresses.

8.6. Compiling a New Kernel

Why would someone want to compile a new kernel? It is often not necessary since the default kernel shipped with Ubuntu handles most configurations. Also, Ubuntu often offers several alternative kernels. So you may want to check first if there is an alternative kernel image package that better corresponds to your hardware. However, it can be useful to compile a new kernel in order to:

- handle special hardware needs, or hardware conflicts with the pre-supplied kernels
- use options of the kernel which are not supported in the pre-supplied kernels (such as high memory support)
- optimize the kernel by removing useless drivers to speed up boot time

- create a monolithic instead of a modularized kernel
- run an updated or development kernel
- learn more about linux kernels

8.6.1. Kernel Image Management

Don't be afraid to try compiling the kernel. It's fun and profitable.

To compile a kernel the Debian/Ubuntu way, you need some packages: `fakeroot`, `kernel-package`, `linux-source-2.6` and a few others which are probably already installed (see `/usr/share/doc/kernel-package/README.gz` for the complete list).

This method will make a .deb of your kernel source, and, if you have non-standard modules, make a synchronized dependent .deb of those too. It's a better way to manage kernel images; `/boot` will hold the kernel, the System.map, and a log of the active config file for the build.

Note that you don't *have* to compile your kernel the "Debian/Ubuntu way"; but we find that using the packaging system to manage your kernel is actually safer and easier. In fact, you can get your kernel sources right from Linus instead of `linux-source-2.6`, yet still use the `kernel-package` compilation method.

Note that you'll find complete documentation on using `kernel-package` under `/usr/share/doc/kernel-package`. This section just contains a brief tutorial.

Hereafter, we'll assume you have free rein over your machine and will extract your kernel source to somewhere in your home directory [18]. We'll also assume that your kernel version is 2.6.28. Make sure you are in the directory to where you want to unpack the kernel sources, extract them using **tar xjf /usr/src/linux-source-2.6.28.tar.bz2** and change to the directory `linux-source-2.6.28` that will have been created.

Now, you can configure your kernel. Run **make xconfig** if X11 is installed, configured and being run; run **make menuconfig** otherwise (you'll need `libncurses5-dev` installed). Take the time to read the online help and choose carefully. When in doubt, it is typically better to include the device driver (the software which manages hardware peripherals, such as Ethernet cards, SCSI controllers, and so on) you are unsure about. Be careful: other options, not related to a specific hardware, should be left at the default value if you do not understand them. Do not forget to select "Kernel module loader" in "Loadable module support" (it is not selected by default). If not included, your Ubuntu installation will experience problems.

---

[18] There are other locations where you can extract kernel sources and build your custom kernel, but this is easiest as it does not require special permissions.

Clean the source tree and reset the `kernel-package` parameters. To do that, do **make-kpkg clean**.

Now, compile the kernel: **fakeroot make-kpkg --initrd --revision=custom.1.0 kernel_image**. The version number of "1.0" can be changed at will; this is just a version number that you will use to track your kernel builds. Likewise, you can put any word you like in place of "custom" (e.g., a host name). Kernel compilation may take quite a while, depending on the power of your machine.

Once the compilation is complete, you can install your custom kernel like any package. As root, do **dpkg -i ../linux-image-2.6.28-*subarchitecture*_custom.1.0_i386.deb**. The *subarchitecture* part is an optional sub-architecture, such as "686", depending on what kernel options you set. **dpkg -i** will install the kernel, along with some other nice supporting files. For instance, the `System.map` will be properly installed (helpful for debugging kernel problems), and `/boot/config-2.6.28` will be installed, containing your current configuration set. Your new kernel package is also clever enough to automatically update your boot loader to use the new kernel. If you have created a modules package, you'll need to install that package as well.

It is time to reboot the system: read carefully any warning that the above step may have produced, then **shutdown -r now**.

For more information on Debian/Ubuntu kernels and kernel compilation, see the *Debian Linux Kernel Handbook*[19]. For more information on `kernel-package`, read the fine documentation in `/usr/share/doc/kernel-package`.

8.7. Recovering a Broken System

Sometimes, things go wrong, and the system you've carefully installed is no longer bootable. Perhaps the boot loader configuration broke while trying out a change, or perhaps a new kernel you installed won't boot, or perhaps cosmic rays hit your disk and flipped a bit in `/sbin/init`. Regardless of the cause, you'll need to have a system to work from while you fix it, and rescue mode can be useful for this.

To access rescue mode, type **rescue** at the `boot:` prompt, or boot with the **rescue/enable=true** boot parameter. You'll be shown the first few screens of the installer, with a note in the corner of the display to indicate that this is rescue mode, not a full installation. Don't worry, your system is not about to be overwritten! Rescue mode simply takes advantage of the hardware detection facilities available in the installer to ensure that your disks, network devices, and so on are available to you while repairing your system.

---

[19] *http://kernel-handbook.alioth.debian.org/*

Instead of the partitioning tool, you should now be presented with a list of the partitions on your system, and asked to select one of them. Normally, you should select the partition containing the root file system that you need to repair. You may select partitions on RAID and LVM devices as well as those created directly on disks.

If possible, the installer will now present you with a shell prompt in the file system you selected, which you can use to perform any necessary repairs. For example, if you need to reinstall the GRUB boot loader into the master boot record of the first hard disk, you could enter the command `grub-install '(hd0)'` to do so.

If the installer cannot run a usable shell in the root file system you selected, perhaps because the file system is corrupt, then it will issue a warning and offer to give you a shell in the installer environment instead. You may not have as many tools available in this environment, but they will often be enough to repair your system anyway. The root file system you selected will be mounted on the `/target` directory.

In either case, after you exit the shell, the system will reboot.

Finally, note that repairing broken systems can be difficult, and this manual does not attempt to go into all the things that might have gone wrong or how to fix them. If you have problems, consult an expert.

Appendix A.
Installation Howto

This document describes how to install Ubuntu 9.10 "Karmic Koala" for the Intel x86 ("i386"). It is a quick walkthrough of the installation process which should contain all the information you will need for most installs. When more information can be useful, we will link to more detailed explanations in other parts of this document.

A.1. Booting the installer

For more information on where to get CDs, see *the section called "Official Ubuntu CD-ROMs"*.

Some installation methods require other images than CD images. *The section called "Where to Find Installation Images"* explains how to find images on Ubuntu mirrors.

The subsections below will give the details about which images you should get for each possible means of installation.

A.1.1. CDROM

Download the image for your architecture and burn it to a CD. To boot the CD, you may need to change your BIOS configuration, as explained in *the section called "Invoking the BIOS Set-Up Menu"*.

A.1.2. USB memory stick

It's also possible to install from removable USB storage devices. For example a USB keychain can make a handy Ubuntu install medium that you can take with you anywhere.

The easiest way to prepare your USB memory stick is to download `netboot/boot.img.gz`, and use gunzip to extract the 8 MB image from that file. Write this image directly to your memory stick, which must be at least 8 MB in size. Of course this will destroy anything already on the memory stick.

There are other, more flexible ways to set up a memory stick to use the Ubuntu installer. For details, see *the section called "Preparing Files for USB Memory Stick Booting"*.

Ubuntu 9.10

Some BIOSes can boot USB storage directly, and some cannot. You may need to configure your BIOS to boot from a "removable drive" or even a "USB-ZIP" to get it to boot from the USB device. For helpful hints and details, see *the section called "Booting from USB Memory Stick"*.

A.1.3. Booting from network

It's also possible to boot the Ubuntu installer completely from the net. The various methods to netboot depend on your architecture and netboot setup. The files in `netboot/` can be used to netboot the Ubuntu installer.

The easiest thing to set up is probably PXE netbooting. Untar the file `netboot/pxeboot.tar.gz` into `/var/lib/tftpboot` or wherever is appropriate for your tftp server. Set up your DHCP server to pass filename `/pxelinux.0` to clients, and with luck everything will just work. For detailed instructions, see *the section called "Preparing Files for TFTP Net Booting"*.

A.2. Installation

Once the installer starts, you will be greeted with an initial screen. Press **Enter** to boot, or read the instructions for other boot methods and parameters (see *the section called "Boot Parameters"*).

After a while you will be asked to select your language. Use the arrow keys to pick a language and press **Enter** to continue. Next you'll be asked to select your country, with the choices including countries where your language is spoken. If it's not on the short list, a list of all the countries in the world is available.

You may be asked to confirm your keyboard layout. Choose the default unless you know better.

Now sit back while the installer detects some of your hardware, and loads the rest of itself from CD, floppy, USB, etc.

Next the installer will try to detect your network hardware and set up networking by DHCP. If you are not on a network or do not have DHCP, you will be given the opportunity to configure the network manually.

The next step is setting up your clock and time zone. The installer will try to contact a time server on the Internet to ensure the clock is set correctly. The time zone is based on the country selected earlier and the installer will only ask to select one if a country has multiple zones.

Now it is time to partition your disks. First you will be given the opportunity to automatically partition either an entire drive, or available free space on a drive (see *the*

Installation Guide

section called "Guided Partitioning"). This is recommended for new users or anyone in a hurry. If you do not want to autopartition, choose Manual from the menu.

If you have an existing DOS or Windows partition that you want to preserve, be very careful with automatic partitioning. If you choose manual partitioning, you can use the installer to resize existing FAT or NTFS partitions to create room for the Ubuntu install: simply select the partition and specify its new size.

If you want to customize the partition layout, choose Manually edit partition table from the menu, and the next screen will show you your partition table, how the partitions will be formatted, and where they will be mounted. Select a partition to modify or delete it. Remember to assign at least one partition for swap space and to mount a partition on /. For more detailed information on how to use the partitioner, please refer to *the section called "Partitioning and Mount Point Selection"*; the appendix *Appendix C, Partitioning for Ubuntu* has more general information about partitioning.

Now the installer formats your partitions and starts to install the base system, which can take a while. That is followed by installing a kernel.

The base system that was installed earlier is a working, but very minimal installation. To make the system more functional the next step allows you to install additional packages by selecting tasks. Before packages can be installed apt needs to be configured as that defines from where the packages will be retrieved. The "Standard system" task will be selected by default and should normally be installed. Select the "Desktop environment" task if you would like to have a graphical desktop after the installation. See *the section called "Selecting and Installing Software"* for additional information about this step.

Installation of the base system is followed by setting up user accounts. By default you will need to provide a password for the "root" (administrator) account and information necessary to create one regular user account.

The last step is to install a boot loader. If the installer detects other operating systems on your computer, it will add them to the boot menu and let you know. By default GRUB will be installed to the master boot record of the first harddrive, which is generally a good choice.

The installer will now tell you that the first stage of installation has finished. Remove the CD and hit **Enter** to reboot your machine. It should boot up into the newly installed system and allow you to log in. This is explained in *Chapter 7, Booting Into Your New Ubuntu System*.

If you need more information on the install process, see *Chapter 6, Using the Ubuntu Installer*.

A.3. And finally...

We hope that your Ubuntu installation is pleasant and that you find Ubuntu useful. You might want to read *Chapter 8, Next Steps and Where to Go From Here*.

Appendix B.
Automating the installation using preseeding

This appendix explains how to preseed answers to questions in `debian-installer` to automate your installation.

The configuration fragments used in this appendix are also available as an example preconfiguration file from *http://help.ubuntu.com/9.10/installation-guide/example-preseed.txt*.

B.1. Introduction

Preseeding provides a way to set answers to questions asked during the installation process, without having to manually enter the answers while the installation is running. This makes it possible to fully automate most types of installation and even offers some features not available during normal installations.

Preseeding is not required. If you use an empty preseed file, the installer will behave just the same way as in a normal manual installation. Each question you preseed will (if you got it right!) modify the installation in some way from that baseline.

B.1.1. Preseeding methods

There are three methods that can be used for preseeding: *initrd*, *file* and *network*. Initrd preseeding will work with any installation method and supports preseeding of more things, but it requires the most preparation. File and network preseeding each can be used with different installation methods.

The following table shows which preseeding methods can be used with which installation methods.

Installation method	initrd	file	network
CD/DVD	yes	yes	yes[a]
netboot	yes	no	yes
hd-media (including usb-stick)	yes	yes	yes[a]
[a] but only if you have network access, and set preseed/url appropriately				

Installation Guide

An important difference between the preseeding methods is the point at which the preconfiguration file is loaded and processed. For initrd preseeding this is right at the start of the installation, before the first question is even asked. For file preseeding this is after the CD or CD image has been loaded. For network preseeding it is only after the network has been configured.

Obviously, any questions that have been processed before the preconfiguration file is loaded cannot be preseeded (this will include questions that are only displayed at medium or low priority, like the first hardware detection run). *The section called "Using boot parameters to preseed questions"* offers a way to avoid these questions being asked.

In order to avoid the questions that would normally appear before the preseeding occurs, you can start the installer in "auto" mode. This delays questions that would normally be asked too early for preseeding (i.e. language, country and keyboard selection) until after the network comes up, thus allowing them to be preseeded. It also runs the installation at critical priority, which avoids many unimportant questions. See *the section called "Auto mode"* for details.

B.1.2. Limitations

Although most questions used by `debian-installer` can be preseeded using this method, there are some notable exceptions. You must (re)partition an entire disk or use available free space on a disk; it is not possible to use existing partitions.

B.2. Using preseeding

You will first need to create a preconfiguration file and place it in the location from where you want to use it. Creating the preconfiguration file is covered later in this appendix. Putting it in the correct location is fairly straightforward for network preseeding or if you want to read the file off a floppy or usb-stick. If you want to include the file on a CD or DVD, you will have to remaster the ISO image. How to get the preconfiguration file included in the initrd is outside the scope of this document; please consult the developers' documentation for `debian-installer`.

An example preconfiguration file that you can use as basis for your own preconfiguration file is available from *http://help.ubuntu.com/9.10/installation-guide/example-preseed.txt*. This file is based on the configuration fragments included in this appendix.

B.2.1. Loading the preconfiguration file

If you are using initrd preseeding, you only have to make sure a file named `preseed.cfg` is included in the root directory of the initrd. The installer will automatically check if this file is present and load it.

Ubuntu 9.10

For the other preseeding methods you need to tell the installer what file to use when you boot it. This is normally done by passing the kernel a boot parameter, either manually at boot time or by editing the bootloader configuration file (e.g. `syslinux.cfg`) and adding the parameter to the end of the append line(s) for the kernel.

If you do specify the preconfiguration file in the bootloader configuration, you might change the configuration so you don't need to hit enter to boot the installer. For syslinux this means setting the timeout to 1 in `syslinux.cfg`.

To make sure the installer gets the right preconfiguration file, you can optionally specify a checksum for the file. Currently this needs to be a md5sum, and if specified it must match the preconfiguration file or the installer will refuse to use it.

```
Boot parameters to specify:
- if you're netbooting:
  preseed/url=http://host/path/to/preseed.cfg
  preseed/url/checksum=5da499872becccfeda2c4872f9171c3d

- if you're booting a remastered CD:
  preseed/file=/cdrom/preseed.cfg
  preseed/file/checksum=5da499872becccfeda2c4872f9171c3d

- if you're installing from USB media (put the preconfiguration file in the
  toplevel directory of the USB stick):
  preseed/file=/hd-media/preseed.cfg
  preseed/file/checksum=5da499872becccfeda2c4872f9171c3d
```

Note that `preseed/url` can be shortened to just `url` and `preseed/file` to just `file` when they are passed as boot parameters.

B.2.2. Using boot parameters to preseed questions

If a preconfiguration file cannot be used to preseed some steps, the install can still be fully automated, since you can pass preseed values on the command line when booting the installer.

Boot parameters can also be used if you do not really want to use preseeding, but just want to provide an answer for a specific question. Some examples where this can be useful are documented elsewhere in this manual.

To set a value to be used inside debian-installer, just pass ***path/to/variable=value*** for any of the preseed variables listed in the examples in this appendix. If a value is to be used to configure packages for the target system, you will need to prepend the *owner*[1] of the

---

[1] The owner of a debconf variable (or template) is normally the name of the package that contains the corresponding debconf template. For variables used in the installer itself the owner is "d-i". Templates and variables can have more than one owner which helps to determine whether they can be removed from the debconf database if the package is purged.

Installation Guide

variable as in *owner:path/to/variable =value*. If you don't specify the owner, the value for the variable will not be copied to the debconf database in the target system and thus remain unused during the configuration of the relevant package.

Normally, preseeding a question in this way will mean that the question will not be asked. To set a specific default value for a question, but still have the question asked, use "?=" instead of "=" as operator. See also *the section called "Using preseeding to change default values"*.

Note that some variables that are frequently set at the boot prompt have a shorter alias. If an alias is available, it is used in the examples in this appendix instead of the full variable. The `preseed/url` variable for example has been aliased as `url`. Another example is the `tasks` alias, which translates to `tasksel:tasksel/first`.

A "--" in the boot options has special meaning. Kernel parameters that appear after the last "--" may be copied into the bootloader configuration for the installed system (if supported by the installer for the bootloader). The installer will automatically filter out any options (like preconfiguration options) that it recognizes.

> **Note**
>
> Current linux kernels (2.6.9 and later) accept a maximum of 32 command line options and 32 environment options, including any options added by default for the installer. If these numbers are exceeded, the kernel will panic (crash). (For earlier kernels, these numbers were lower.)

For most installations some of the default options in your bootloader configuration file, like `vga=normal`, may be safely removed which may allow you to add more options for preseeding.

> **Note**
>
> It may not always be possible to specify values with spaces for boot parameters, even if you delimit them with quotes.

B.2.3. Auto mode

There are several features of Debian Installer that combine to allow fairly simple command lines at the boot prompt to result in arbitrarily complex customized automatic installs. To illustrate this, here are some examples that can be used at the boot prompt:

```
auto url=autoserver
```

This relies on there being a DHCP server that will get the machine to the point where `autoserver` can be resolved by DNS, perhaps after adding the local domain if that was provided by DHCP. If this was done at a site where the domain is `example.com`, and they

123

have a reasonably sane DHCP setup, it would result in the preseed file being retrieved from `http://autoserver.example.com/d-i/jaunty/./preseed.cfg`.

The last part of that url (`d-i/jaunty/./preseed.cfg`) is taken from `auto-install/defaultroot`. By default this includes the directory `jaunty` to allow future versions to specify their own codename and let people migrate forwards in a controlled manner. The `/./` bit is used to indicate a root, relative to which subsequent paths can be anchored (for use in preseed/include and preseed/run). This allows files to be specified either as full URLs, paths starting with / that are thus anchored, or even paths relative to the location where the last preseed file was found. This can be used to construct more portable scripts where an entire hierarchy of scripts can be moved to a new location without breaking it, for example copying the files onto a USB stick when they started out on a web server. In this example, if the preseed file sets `preseed/run` to `/scripts/late_command.sh` then the file will be fetched from `http://autoserver.example.com/d-i/jaunty/./scripts/late_command.sh`.

If there is no local DHCP or DNS infrastructure, or if you do not want to use the default path to `preseed.cfg`, you can still use an explicit url, and if you don't use the `/./` element it will be anchored to the start of the path (i.e. the third / in the URL). Here is an example that requires minimal support from the local network infrastructure:

```
auto url=http://192.168.1.2/path/to/mypreseed.file
```

The way this works is that:

- if the URL is missing a protocol, http is assumed,
- if the hostname section contains no periods, it has the domain derived from DHCP appended to it, and
- if there's no /'s after the hostname, then the default path is added.

In addition to specifying the url, you can also specify settings that do not directly affect the behavior of `debian-installer` itself, but can be passed through to scripts specified using `preseed/run` in the loaded preseed file. At present, the only example of this is `auto-install/classes`, which has an alias `classes`. This can be used thus:

```
auto url=example.com classes=class_A;class_B
```

The classes could for example denote the type of system to be installed, or the localization to be used.

It is of course possible to extend this concept, and if you do, it is reasonable to use the auto-install namespace for this. So one might have something like `auto-install/style` which is then used in your scripts. If you feel the need to do this, please mention it on the `<debian-boot@lists.debian.org>` mailing list so that we can avoid namespace conflicts, and perhaps add an alias for the parameter for you.

Installation Guide

The `auto` boot label is not yet defined on all architectures. The same effect may be achieved by simply adding the two parameters `auto=true priority=critical` to the kernel command line. The `auto` parameter is an alias for `auto-install/enable` and controls the delay of the locale and keyboard questions until after there has been a chance to preseed them, while `priority` is an alias for `debconf/priority` and setting it to `critical` stops any questions with a lower priority from being asked.

Additional options that may be of interest while attempting to automate an install while using DHCP are: `interface=auto netcfg/dhcp_timeout=60` which makes the machine choose the first viable NIC and be more patient about getting a reply to its DHCP query.

> **Tip**
>
> An extensive example of how to use this framework, including example scripts and classes, can be found on the *website of its developer*[2]. The examples available there also show many other nice effects that can be achieved by creative use of preconfiguration.

B.2.4. Aliases useful with preseeding

The following aliases can be useful when using (auto mode) preseeding.

auto	auto-install/enable
classes	auto-install/classes
fb	debian-installer/framebuffer
locale	debian-installer/locale
priority	debconf/priority
file	preseed/file
url	preseed/url
interface	netcfg/choose_interface
hostname	netcfg/get_hostname
domain	netcfg/get_domain
protocol	mirror/protocol
suite	mirror/suite

---

[2] *http://hands.com/d-i/*

B.2.5. Using a DHCP server to specify preconfiguration files

It's also possible to use DHCP to specify a preconfiguration file to download from the network. DHCP allows specifying a filename. Normally this is a file to netboot, but if it appears to be an URL then installation media that support network preseeding will download the file from the URL and use it as a preconfiguration file. Here is an example of how to set it up in the dhcpd.conf for version 3 of the ISC DHCP server (the dhcp3-server Ubuntu package).

```
if substring (option vendor-class-identifier, 0, 3) = "d-i" {
    filename "http://host/preseed.cfg";
}
```

Note that the above example limits this filename to DHCP clients that identify themselves as "d-i", so it will not affect regular DHCP clients, but only the installer. You can also put the text in a stanza for only one particular host to avoid preseeding all installs on your network.

A good way to use the DHCP preseeding is to only preseed values specific to your network, such as the Ubuntu mirror to use. This way installs on your network will automatically get a good mirror selected, but the rest of the installation can be performed interactively. Using DHCP preseeding to fully automate Ubuntu installs should only be done with care.

B.3. Creating a preconfiguration file

The preconfiguration file is in the format used by the **debconf-set-selections** command. The general format of a line in a preconfiguration file is:

```
<owner> <question name> <question type> <value>
```

There are a few rules to keep in mind when writing a preconfiguration file.

- Put only a single space or tab between type and value: any additional whitespace will be interpreted as belonging to the value.
- A line can be split into multiple lines by appending a backslash ("\") as the line continuation character. A good place to split a line is after the question name; a bad place is between type and value. Split lines will be joined into a single line with all leading/trailing whitespace condensed to a single space.
- For debconf variables (templates) used in the installer itself, the owner should be set to "d-i"; to preseed variables used in the installed system, the name of the package that contains the corresponding debconf template should be used. Only variables that have their owner set to something other than "d-i" will be propagated to the debconf database for the installed system.
- Most questions need to be preseeded using the values valid in English and not the translated values. However, there are some questions (for example in `partman`) where the translated values need to be used.

- Some questions take a code as value instead of the English text that is shown during installation.

The easiest way to create a preconfiguration file is to use the example file linked in *the section called "Contents of the preconfiguration file (for jaunty)"* as basis and work from there.

An alternative method is to do a manual installation and then, after rebooting, use the **debconf-get-selections** from the `debconf-utils` package to dump both the debconf database and the installer's cdebconf database to a single file:

```
$ debconf-get-selections --installer > file
$ debconf-get-selections >> file
```

However, a file generated in this manner will have some items that should not be preseeded, and the example file is a better starting place for most users.

> **Note**
>
> This method relies on the fact that, at the end of the installation, the installer's cdebconf database is saved to the installed system in `/var/log/installer/cdebconf`. However, because the database may contain sensitive information, by default the files are only readable by root.
>
> The directory `/var/log/installer` and all files in it will be deleted from your system if you purge the package `installation-report`.

To check possible values for questions, you can use **nano** to examine the files in `/var/lib/cdebconf` while an installation is in progress. View `templates.dat` for the raw templates and `questions.dat` for the current values and for the values assigned to variables.

To check if the format of your preconfiguration file is valid before performing an install, you can use the command **debconf-set-selections** -c *preseed.cfg*.

B.4. Contents of the preconfiguration file (for jaunty)

The configuration fragments used in this appendix are also available as an example preconfiguration file from *http://help.ubuntu.com/9.10/installation-guide/example-preseed.txt*.

Note that this example is based on an installation for the Intel x86 architecture. If you are installing a different architecture, some of the examples (like keyboard selection and bootloader installation) may not be relevant and will need to be replaced by debconf settings appropriate for your architecture.

B.4.1. Localization

Setting localization values will only work if you are using initrd preseeding. With all other methods the preconfiguration file will only be loaded after these questions have been asked.

Ubuntu 9.10

The locale can be used to specify both language and country and can be any combination of a language supported by `debian-installer` and a recognized country. If the combination does not form a valid locale, the installer will automatically select a locale that is valid for the selected language. To specify the locale as a boot parameter, use **locale= en_US**.

```
# Locale sets language and country.
d-i debian-installer/locale string en_US
```

Keyboard configuration consists of selecting a keyboard architecture and a keymap. In most cases the correct keyboard architecture is selected by default, so there's normally no need to preseed it. The keymap must be known to the `debian-installer` for the selected keyboard architecture.

To specify the keymap as a boot parameter, use **console-setup/ask_detect=false console-setup/layoutcode= us**. The layout code is an X layout name, as would be used in the **XkbLayout** option in `/etc/X11/xorg.conf`.

```
# Keyboard selection.
# Disable automatic (interactive) keymap detection.
d-i console-setup/ask_detect boolean false
#d-i console-setup/modelcode string pc105
d-i console-setup/layoutcode string us
# To select a variant of the selected layout (if you leave this out, the
# basic form of the layout will be used):
#d-i console-setup/variantcode string dvorak
```

To skip keyboard configuration, preseed `console-setup/modelcode` with **SKIP**. This will result in the kernel keymap remaining active.

> **Note**
>
> The changes in the input layer for 2.6 kernels have made the keyboard architecture virtually obsolete. For 2.6 kernels normally a "PC" (**pc105**) model should be selected.

B.4.2. Network configuration

Of course, preseeding the network configuration won't work if you're loading your preconfiguration file from the network. But it's great when you're booting from CD or USB stick. If you are loading preconfiguration files from the network, you can pass network config parameters by using kernel boot parameters.

If you need to pick a particular interface when netbooting before loading a preconfiguration file from the network, use a boot parameter such as **interface= eth1**.

Although preseeding the network configuration is normally not possible when using network preseeding (using "preseed/url"), you can use the following hack to work around that, for example if you'd like to set a static address for the network interface. The hack is to

Installation Guide

force the network configuration to run again after the preconfiguration file has been loaded by creating a "preseed/run" script containing the following commands:

```
killall.sh; netcfg
```

The following debconf variables are relevant for network configuration.

```
# netcfg will choose an interface that has link if possible. This makes it
# skip displaying a list if there is more than one interface.
d-i netcfg/choose_interface select auto

# To pick a particular interface instead:
#d-i netcfg/choose_interface select eth1

# If you have a slow dhcp server and the installer times out waiting for
# it, this might be useful.
#d-i netcfg/dhcp_timeout string 60

# If you prefer to configure the network manually, uncomment this line and
# the static network configuration below.
#d-i netcfg/disable_dhcp boolean true

# If you want the preconfiguration file to work on systems both with and
# without a dhcp server, uncomment these lines and the static network
# configuration below.
#d-i netcfg/dhcp_failed note
#d-i netcfg/dhcp_options select Configure network manually

# Static network configuration.
#d-i netcfg/get_nameservers string 192.168.1.1
#d-i netcfg/get_ipaddress string 192.168.1.42
#d-i netcfg/get_netmask string 255.255.255.0
#d-i netcfg/get_gateway string 192.168.1.1
#d-i netcfg/confirm_static boolean true

# Any hostname and domain names assigned from dhcp take precedence over
# values set here. However, setting the values still prevents the questions
# from being shown, even if values come from dhcp.
d-i netcfg/get_hostname string unassigned-hostname
d-i netcfg/get_domain string unassigned-domain

# Disable that annoying WEP key dialog.
d-i netcfg/wireless_wep string
# The wacky dhcp hostname that some ISPs use as a password of sorts.
#d-i netcfg/dhcp_hostname string radish

# If non-free firmware is needed for the network or other hardware, you can
# configure the installer to always try to load it, without prompting. Or
# change to false to disable asking.
#d-i hw-detect/load_firmware boolean true
```

Please note that **netcfg** will automatically determine the netmask if `netcfg/get_netmask` is not preseeded. In this case, the variable has to be marked as `seen` for automatic installations.

Similarly, **netcfg** will choose an appropriate address if `netcfg/get_gateway` is not set. As a special case, you can set `netcfg/get_gateway` to "none" to specify that no gateway should be used.

B.4.3. Mirror settings

Depending on the installation method you use, a mirror may be used to download additional components of the installer, to install the base system, and to set up the `/etc/apt/sources.list` for the installed system.

The parameter `mirror/suite` determines the suite for the installed system.

The parameter `mirror/udeb/suite` determines the suite for additional components for the installer. It is only useful to set this if components are actually downloaded over the network and should match the suite that was used to build the initrd for the installation method used for the installation. By default the value for `mirror/udeb/suite` is the same as `mirror/suite`.

The parameter `mirror/udeb/components` determines the archive components from which additional installer components are fetched. It is only useful to set this if components are actually downloaded over the network. The default components are main and restricted.

```
# If you select ftp, the mirror/country string does not need to be set.
#d-i mirror/protocol string ftp
d-i mirror/country string manual
d-i mirror/http/hostname string archive.ubuntu.com
d-i mirror/http/directory string /ubuntu
d-i mirror/http/proxy string

# Alternatively: by default, the installer uses CC.archive.ubuntu.com where
# CC is the ISO-3166-2 code for the selected country. You can preseed this
# so that it does so without asking.
#d-i mirror/http/mirror select CC.archive.ubuntu.com

# Suite to install.
#d-i mirror/suite string jaunty
# Suite to use for loading installer components (optional).
#d-i mirror/udeb/suite string jaunty
# Components to use for loading installer components (optional).
#d-i mirror/udeb/components multiselect main, restricted
```

B.4.4. Clock and time zone setup

```
# Controls whether or not the hardware clock is set to UTC.
d-i clock-setup/utc boolean true

# You may set this to any valid setting for $TZ; see the contents of
# /usr/share/zoneinfo/ for valid values.
d-i time/zone string US/Eastern
```

Installation Guide

```
# Controls whether to use NTP to set the clock during the install
d-i clock-setup/ntp boolean true
# NTP server to use. The default is almost always fine here.
#d-i clock-setup/ntp-server string ntp.example.com
```

B.4.5. Partitioning

Using preseeding to partition the harddisk is very much limited to what is supported by `partman-auto`. You can choose to partition either existing free space on a disk or a whole disk. The layout of the disk can be determined by using a predefined recipe, a custom recipe from a recipe file or a recipe included in the preconfiguration file. It is currently not possible to partition multiple disks using preseeding.

> ⚠️ **Warning**
>
> The identification of disks is dependent on the order in which their drivers are loaded. If there are multiple disks in the system, make very sure the correct one will be selected before using preseeding.

```
# If the system has free space you can choose to only partition that space.
# Alternatives: custom, some_device, some_device_crypto, some_device_lvm.
#d-i partman-auto/init_automatically_partition select biggest_free

# Alternatively, you can specify a disk to partition. The device name must
# be given in traditional non-devfs format.
# Note: A disk must be specified, unless the system has only one disk.
# For example, to use the first SCSI/SATA hard disk:
#d-i partman-auto/disk string /dev/sda
# In addition, you'll need to specify the method to use.
# The presently available methods are: "regular", "lvm" and "crypto"
d-i partman-auto/method string lvm

# If one of the disks that are going to be automatically partitioned
# contains an old LVM configuration, the user will normally receive a
# warning. This can be preseeded away...
d-i partman-lvm/device_remove_lvm boolean true
# The same applies to pre-existing software RAID array:
d-i partman-md/device_remove_md boolean true
# And the same goes for the confirmation to write the lvm partitions.
d-i partman-lvm/confirm boolean true

# For LVM partitioning, you can select how much of the volume group to use
# for logical volumes.
#d-i partman-auto-lvm/guided_size string max
#d-i partman-auto-lvm/guided_size string 10GB
#d-i partman-auto-lvm/guided_size string 50%

# You can choose one of the three predefined partitioning recipes:
# - atomic: all files in one partition
# - home:   separate /home partition
# - multi:  separate /home, /usr, /var, and /tmp partitions
d-i partman-auto/choose_recipe select atomic
```

131

Ubuntu 9.10

```
# Or provide a recipe of your own...
# The recipe format is documented in the file devel/partman-auto-recipe.txt.
# If you have a way to get a recipe file into the d-i environment, you can
# just point at it.
#d-i partman-auto/expert_recipe_file string /hd-media/recipe

# If not, you can put an entire recipe into the preconfiguration file in one
# (logical) line. This example creates a small /boot partition, suitable
# swap, and uses the rest of the space for the root partition:
#d-i partman-auto/expert_recipe string                         \
#      boot-root ::                                            \
#              40 50 100 ext3                                  \
#                      $primary{ } $bootable{ }                \
#                      method{ format } format{ }              \
#                      use_filesystem{ } filesystem{ ext3 }    \
#                      mountpoint{ /boot }                     \
#              .                                               \
#              500 10000 1000000000 ext3                       \
#                      method{ format } format{ }              \
#                      use_filesystem{ } filesystem{ ext3 }    \
#                      mountpoint{ / }                         \
#              .                                               \
#              64 512 300% linux-swap                          \
#                      method{ swap } format{ }                \
#              .

# If you just want to change the default filesystem from ext3 to something
# else, you can do that without providing a full recipe.
#d-i partman/default_filesystem string ext4

# This makes partman automatically partition without confirmation, provided
# that you told it what to do using one of the methods above.
d-i partman/confirm_write_new_label boolean true
d-i partman/choose_partition select finish
d-i partman/confirm boolean true
```

B.4.6. Partitioning using RAID

You can also use preseeding to set up partitions on software RAID arrays. Supported are RAID levels 0, 1, 5, 6 and 10, creating degraded arrays and specifying spare devices. If you are using RAID 1, you can preseed grub to install to all devices used in the array; see *the section called "Boot loader installation"*.

> **Warning**
>
> This type of automated partitioning is easy to get wrong. It is also functionality that receives relatively little testing from the developers of debian-installer. The responsibility to get the various recipes right (so they make sense and don't conflict) lies with the user. Check /var/log/syslog if you run into problems.

```
# NOTE: this option is of beta release quality and should be used carefully

# The method should be set to "raid".
```

Installation Guide

```
#d-i partman-auto/method string raid
# Specify the disks to be partitioned. They will all get the same layout,
# so this will only work if the disks are the same size.
#d-i partman-auto/disk string /dev/discs/disc0/disc /dev/discs/disc1/disc

# Next you need to specify the physical partitions that will be used.
#d-i partman-auto/expert_recipe string \
#      multiraid ::                                                \
#              1000 5000 4000 raid                                 \
#                      $primary{ } method{ raid }                  \
#              .                                                   \
#              64 512 300% raid                                    \
#                      method{ raid }                              \
#              .                                                   \
#              500 10000 1000000000 raid                           \
#                      method{ raid }                              \
#              .

# Last you need to specify how the previously defined partitions will be
# used in the RAID setup. Remember to use the correct partition numbers
# for logical partitions.
# Parameters are:
# <raidtype> <devcount> <sparecount> <fstype> <mountpoint> \
#          <devices> <sparedevices>
# RAID levels 0, 1, 5, 6 and 10 are supported; devices are separated using "#"
#d-i partman-auto-raid/recipe string \
#    1 2 0 ext3 /                                                  \
#          /dev/discs/disc0/part1#/dev/discs/disc1/part1           \
#    .                                                             \
#    1 2 0 swap -                                                  \
#          /dev/discs/disc0/part5#/dev/discs/disc1/part5           \
#    .                                                             \
#    0 2 0 ext3 /home                                              \
#          /dev/discs/disc0/part6#/dev/discs/disc1/part6           \
#    .

# This makes partman automatically partition without confirmation.
d-i partman-md/confirm boolean true
d-i partman/confirm_write_new_label boolean true
d-i partman/choose_partition select finish
d-i partman/confirm boolean true
```

B.4.7. Controlling how partitions are mounted

Normally, filesystems are mounted using a universally unique identifier (UUID) as a key; this allows them to be mounted properly even if their device name changes. UUIDs are long and difficult to read, so, if you prefer, the installer can mount filesystems based on the traditional device names, or based on a label you assign. If you ask the installer to mount by label, any filesystems without a label will be mounted using a UUID instead.

Devices with stable names, such as LVM logical volumes, will continue to use their traditional names rather than UUIDs.

Ubuntu 9.10

> ⚠ **Warning**
> Traditional device names may change based on the order in which the kernel discovers devices at boot, which may cause the wrong filesystem to be mounted. Similarly, labels are likely to clash if you plug in a new disk or a USB drive, and if that happens your system's behaviour when started will be random.

```
# The default is to mount by UUID, but you can also choose "traditional" to
# use traditional device names, or "label" to try filesystem labels before
# falling back to UUIDs.
#d-i partman/mount_style select uuid
```

B.4.8. Base system installation

There is actually not very much that can be preseeded for this stage of the installation. The only questions asked concern the installation of the kernel.

```
# Select the initramfs generator used to generate the initrd for 2.6 kernels.
#d-i base-installer/kernel/linux/initramfs-generators string yaird

# The kernel image (meta) package to be installed; "none" can be used if no
# kernel is to be installed.
#d-i base-installer/kernel/image string linux-generic
```

B.4.9. Account setup

The password for the root account and name and password for a first regular user's account can be preseeded. For the passwords you can use either clear text values or MD5 *hashes*.

> ⚠ **Warning**
> Be aware that preseeding passwords is not completely secure as everyone with access to the preconfiguration file will have the knowledge of these passwords. Using MD5 hashes is considered slightly better in terms of security but it might also give a false sense of security as access to a MD5 hash allows for brute force attacks.

```
# Skip creation of a root account (normal user account will be able to use sudo).
# The default is false; preseed this to true if you want to set a root password.
#d-i passwd/root-login boolean false
# Alternatively, to skip creation of a normal user account.
#d-i passwd/make-user boolean false

# Root password, either in clear text
#d-i passwd/root-password password r00tme
#d-i passwd/root-password-again password r00tme
# or encrypted using an MD5 hash.
#d-i passwd/root-password-crypted password [MD5 hash]

# To create a normal user account.
#d-i passwd/user-fullname string Ubuntu User
#d-i passwd/username string ubuntu
```

Installation Guide

```
# Normal user's password, either in clear text
#d-i passwd/user-password password insecure
#d-i passwd/user-password-again password insecure
# or encrypted using an MD5 hash.
#d-i passwd/user-password-crypted password [MD5 hash]
# Create the first user with the specified UID instead of the default.
#d-i passwd/user-uid string 1010
# The installer will warn about weak passwords. If you are sure you know
# what you're doing and want to override it, uncomment this.
#d-i user-setup/allow-password-weak boolean true

# The user account will be added to some standard initial groups. To
# override that, use this.
#d-i passwd/user-default-groups string audio cdrom video

# Set to true if you want to encrypt the first user's home directory.
d-i user-setup/encrypt-home boolean false
```

The `passwd/root-password-crypted` and `passwd/user-password-crypted` variables can also be preseeded with "!" as their value. In that case, the corresponding account is disabled. This may be convenient for the root account, provided of course that an alternative method is set up to allow administrative activities or root login (for instance by using SSH key authentication or **sudo**).

The following command can be used to generate an MD5 hash for a password:

```
$ echo "r00tme" | mkpasswd -s -m md5
```

B.4.10. Apt setup

Setup of the `/etc/apt/sources.list` and basic configuration options is fully automated based on your installation method and answers to earlier questions. You can optionally add other (local) repositories.

```
# You can choose to install restricted and universe software, or to install
# software from the backports repository.
#d-i apt-setup/restricted boolean true
#d-i apt-setup/universe boolean true
#d-i apt-setup/backports boolean true
# Uncomment this if you don't want to use a network mirror.
#d-i apt-setup/use_mirror boolean false
# Select which update services to use; define the mirrors to be used.
# Values shown below are the normal defaults.
#d-i apt-setup/services-select multiselect security
#d-i apt-setup/security_host string security.ubuntu.com
#d-i apt-setup/security_path string /ubuntu

# Additional repositories, local[0-9] available
#d-i apt-setup/local0/repository string \
#       http://local.server/ubuntu jaunty main
#d-i apt-setup/local0/comment string local server
```

135

Ubuntu 9.10

```
# Enable deb-src lines
#d-i apt-setup/local0/source boolean true
# URL to the public key of the local repository; you must provide a key or
# apt will complain about the unauthenticated repository and so the
# sources.list line will be left commented out
#d-i apt-setup/local0/key string http://local.server/key

# By default the installer requires that repositories be authenticated
# using a known gpg key. This setting can be used to disable that
# authentication. Warning: Insecure, not recommended.
#d-i debian-installer/allow_unauthenticated string true
```

B.4.11. Package selection

You can choose to install any combination of tasks that are available. Available tasks as of this writing include:

- `standard`
- `ubuntu-desktop`
- `kubuntu-desktop`
- `edubuntu-desktop`
- `xubuntu-desktop`
- `dns-server`
- `lamp-server`

You can also choose to install no tasks, and force the installation of a set of packages in some other way. We recommend always including the `standard` task.

If you want to install some individual packages in addition to packages installed by tasks, you can use the parameter `pkgsel/include`. The value of this parameter can be a list of packages separated by either commas or spaces, which allows it to be used easily on the kernel command line as well. By default, recommended packages will not be installed; to change this, preseed `pkgsel/install-recommends` to true.

To install a different set of language packs, you can use the parameter `pkgsel/language-packs`. The value of this parameter should be a list of ISO-639 language codes. If not set, the language packs matching the language selected in the installer will be installed.

```
tasksel tasksel/first multiselect ubuntu-desktop
#tasksel tasksel/first multiselect lamp-server, print-server
#tasksel tasksel/first multiselect kubuntu-desktop

# Individual additional packages to install
#d-i pkgsel/include string openssh-server build-essential
# Whether to upgrade packages after debootstrap.
# Allowed values: none, safe-upgrade, full-upgrade
#d-i pkgsel/upgrade select none

# Language pack selection
```

Installation Guide

```
#d-i pkgsel/language-packs multiselect de, en, zh

# Policy for applying updates. May be "none" (no automatic updates),
# "unattended-upgrades" (install security updates automatically), or
# "landscape" (manage system with Landscape).
#d-i pkgsel/update-policy select none

# Some versions of the installer can report back on what software you have
# installed, and what software you use. The default is not to report back,
# but sending reports helps the project determine what software is most
# popular and include it on CDs.
#popularity-contest popularity-contest/participate boolean false

# By default, the system's locate database will be updated after the
# installer has finished installing most packages. This may take a while, so
# if you don't want it, you can set this to "false" to turn it off.
#d-i pkgsel/updatedb boolean true
```

B.4.12. Boot loader installation

```
# Grub is the default boot loader (for x86). If you want lilo installed
# instead, uncomment this:
#d-i grub-installer/skip boolean true
# To also skip installing lilo, and install no bootloader, uncomment this
# too:
#d-i lilo-installer/skip boolean true

# This is fairly safe to set, it makes grub install automatically to the MBR
# if no other operating system is detected on the machine.
d-i grub-installer/only_debian boolean true

# This one makes grub-installer install to the MBR if it also finds some other
# OS, which is less safe as it might not be able to boot that other OS.
d-i grub-installer/with_other_os boolean true

# Alternatively, if you want to install to a location other than the mbr,
# uncomment and edit these lines:
#d-i grub-installer/only_debian boolean false
#d-i grub-installer/with_other_os boolean false
#d-i grub-installer/bootdev  string (hd0,0)
# To install grub to multiple disks:
#d-i grub-installer/bootdev  string (hd0,0) (hd1,0) (hd2,0)

# Optional password for grub, either in clear text
#d-i grub-installer/password password r00tme
#d-i grub-installer/password-again password r00tme
# or encrypted using an MD5 hash, see grub-md5-crypt(8).
#d-i grub-installer/password-crypted password [MD5 hash]
```

An MD5 hash for a password for grub can be generated using **grub-md5-crypt**, or using the command from the example in *the section called "Account setup"*.

Ubuntu 9.10

B.4.13. Finishing up the installation

```
# During installations from serial console, the regular virtual consoles
# (VT1-VT6) are normally disabled in /etc/inittab. Uncomment the next
# line to prevent this.
#d-i finish-install/keep-consoles boolean true

# Avoid that last message about the install being complete.
d-i finish-install/reboot_in_progress note

# This will prevent the installer from ejecting the CD during the reboot,
# which is useful in some situations.
#d-i cdrom-detect/eject boolean false

# This is how to make the installer shutdown when finished, but not
# reboot into the installed system.
#d-i debian-installer/exit/halt boolean true
# This will power off the machine instead of just halting it.
#d-i debian-installer/exit/poweroff boolean true
```

B.4.14. X configuration

Preseeding Ubuntu's X config is possible, but you probably need to know some details about the video hardware of the machine, since Ubuntu's X configurator does not do fully automatic configuration of everything.

```
# X can detect the right driver for some cards, but if you're preseeding,
# you override whatever it chooses. Still, vesa will work most places.
#xserver-xorg xserver-xorg/config/device/driver select vesa

# A caveat with mouse autodetection is that if it fails, X will retry it
# over and over. So if it's preseeded to be done, there is a possibility of
# an infinite loop if the mouse is not autodetected.
#xserver-xorg xserver-xorg/autodetect_mouse boolean true

# Monitor autodetection is recommended.
xserver-xorg xserver-xorg/autodetect_monitor boolean true
# Uncomment if you have an LCD display.
#xserver-xorg xserver-xorg/config/monitor/lcd boolean true
# X has three configuration paths for the monitor. Here's how to preseed
# the "medium" path, which is always available. The "simple" path may not
# be available, and the "advanced" path asks too many questions.
xserver-xorg xserver-xorg/config/monitor/selection-method \
       select medium
xserver-xorg xserver-xorg/config/monitor/mode-list \
       select 1024x768 @ 60 Hz
```

B.4.15. Preseeding other packages

```
# Depending on what software you choose to install, or if things go wrong
# during the installation process, it's possible that other questions may
# be asked. You can preseed those too, of course. To get a list of every
# possible question that could be asked during an install, do an
```

```
# installation, and then run these commands:
#   debconf-get-selections --installer > file
#   debconf-get-selections >> file
```

B.5. Advanced options

B.5.1. Running custom commands during the installation

A very powerful and flexible option offered by the preconfiguration tools is the ability to run commands or scripts at certain points in the installation.

```
# d-i preseeding is inherently not secure. Nothing in the installer checks
# for attempts at buffer overflows or other exploits of the values of a
# preconfiguration file like this one. Only use preconfiguration files from
# trusted locations! To drive that home, and because it's generally useful,
# here's a way to run any shell command you'd like inside the installer,
# automatically.

# This first command is run as early as possible, just after
# preseeding is read.
#d-i preseed/early_command string anna-install some-udeb

# This command is run immediately before the partitioner starts. It may be
# useful to apply dynamic partitioner preseeding that depends on the state
# of the disks (which may not be visible when preseed/early_command runs).
#d-i partman/early_command string debconf-set partman-auto/disk "$(list-devices disk | head -n1)"

# This command is run just before the install finishes, but when there is
# still a usable /target directory. You can chroot to /target and use it
# directly, or use the apt-install and in-target commands to easily install
# packages and run commands in the target system.
#d-i preseed/late_command string apt-install zsh; in-target chsh -s /bin/zsh
```

B.5.2. Using preseeding to change default values

It is possible to use preseeding to change the default answer for a question, but still have the question asked. To do this the *seen* flag must be reset to "false" after setting the value for a question.

```
d-i foo/bar string value
d-i foo/bar seen false
```

The same effect can be achieved for *all* questions by setting the parameter `preseed/interactive=true` at the boot prompt. This can also be useful for testing or debugging your preconfiguration file.

If you are preseeding using boot parameters, you can make the installer ask the corresponding question by using the "?=" operator, i.e. *foo/bar?= value*. This will of course only have effect for parameters that correspond to questions that are actually displayed during an installation and not for "internal" parameters.

B.5.3. Chainloading preconfiguration files

It is possible to include other preconfiguration files from a preconfiguration file. Any settings in those files will override pre-existing settings from files loaded earlier. This makes it possible to put, for example, general networking settings for your location in one file and more specific settings for certain configurations in other files.

```
# More than one file can be listed, separated by spaces; all will be
# loaded. The included files can have preseed/include directives of their
# own as well. Note that if the filenames are relative, they are taken from
# the same directory as the preconfiguration file that includes them.
#d-i preseed/include string x.cfg

# The installer can optionally verify checksums of preconfiguration files
# before using them. Currently only md5sums are supported, list the md5sums
# in the same order as the list of files to include.
#d-i preseed/include/checksum string 5da499872becccfeda2c4872f9171c3d

# More flexibly, this runs a shell command and if it outputs the names of
# preconfiguration files, includes those files.
#d-i preseed/include_command \
#      string if [ "`hostname`" = bob ]; then echo bob.cfg; fi

# Most flexibly of all, this downloads a program and runs it. The program
# can use commands such as debconf-set to manipulate the debconf database.
# More than one script can be listed, separated by spaces.
# Note that if the filenames are relative, they are taken from the same
# directory as the preconfiguration file that runs them.
#d-i preseed/run string foo.sh
```

It is also possible to chainload from the initrd or file preseeding phase, into network preseeding by setting preseed/url in the earlier files. This will cause network preseeding to be performed when the network comes up. You need to be careful when doing this, since there will be two distinct runs at preseeding, meaning for example that you get another chance to run the preseed/early command, the second one happening after the network comes up.

Appendix C.
Partitioning for Ubuntu

C.1. Deciding on Ubuntu Partitions and Sizes

At a bare minimum, GNU/Linux needs one partition for itself. You can have a single partition containing the entire operating system, applications, and your personal files. Most people feel that a separate swap partition is also a necessity, although it's not strictly true. "Swap" is scratch space for an operating system, which allows the system to use disk storage as "virtual memory". By putting swap on a separate partition, Linux can make much more efficient use of it. It is possible to force Linux to use a regular file as swap, but it is not recommended.

Most people choose to give GNU/Linux more than the minimum number of partitions, however. There are two reasons you might want to break up the file system into a number of smaller partitions. The first is for safety. If something happens to corrupt the file system, generally only one partition is affected. Thus, you only have to replace (from the backups you've been carefully keeping) a portion of your system. At a bare minimum, you should consider creating what is commonly called a "root partition". This contains the most essential components of the system. If any other partitions get corrupted, you can still boot into GNU/Linux to fix the system. This can save you the trouble of having to reinstall the system from scratch.

The second reason is generally more important in a business setting, but it really depends on your use of the machine. For example, a mail server getting spammed with e-mail can easily fill a partition. If you made /var/mail a separate partition on the mail server, most of the system will remain working even if you get spammed.

The only real drawback to using more partitions is that it is often difficult to know in advance what your needs will be. If you make a partition too small then you will either have to reinstall the system or you will be constantly moving things around to make room in the undersized partition. On the other hand, if you make the partition too big, you will be wasting space that could be used elsewhere. Disk space is cheap nowadays, but why throw your money away?

C.2. The Directory Tree

Ubuntu adheres to the *Filesystem Hierarchy Standard*[1] for directory and file naming. This standard allows users and software programs to predict the location of files and directories. The root level directory is represented simply by the slash /. At the root level, all Ubuntu systems include these directories:

Directory	Content
bin	Essential command binaries
boot	Static files of the boot loader
dev	Device files
etc	Host-specific system configuration
home	User home directories
lib	Essential shared libraries and kernel modules
media	Contains mount points for replaceable media
mnt	Mount point for mounting a file system temporarily
proc	Virtual directory for system information (2.4 and 2.6 kernels)
root	Home directory for the root user
sbin	Essential system binaries
sys	Virtual directory for system information (2.6 kernels)
tmp	Temporary files
usr	Secondary hierarchy
var	Variable data
srv	Data for services provided by the system
opt	Add-on application software packages

The following is a list of important considerations regarding directories and partitions. Note that disk usage varies widely given system configuration and specific usage patterns. The recommendations here are general guidelines and provide a starting point for partitioning.

- The root partition / must always physically contain /etc, /bin, /sbin, /lib and /dev, otherwise you won't be able to boot. Typically 150–250MB is needed for the root partition.

---

[1] *http://www.pathname.com/fhs/*

Installation Guide

- `/usr`: contains all user programs (`/usr/bin`), libraries (`/usr/lib`), documentation (`/usr/share/doc`), etc. This is the part of the file system that generally takes up most space. You should provide at least 500MB of disk space. This amount should be increased depending on the number and type of packages you plan to install. A standard Ubuntu desktop requires a minimum of 1.5GB here. A generous workstation or server installation should allow 4–6GB.

- `/var`: variable data like news articles, e-mails, web sites, databases, the packaging system cache, etc. will be placed under this directory. The size of this directory depends greatly on the usage of your system, but for most people will be dictated by the package management tool's overhead. If you are going to do a full installation of just about everything Ubuntu has to offer, all in one session, setting aside 2 or 3 GB of space for `/var` should be sufficient. If you are going to install in pieces (that is to say, install services and utilities, followed by text stuff, then X, ...), you can get away with 300–500 MB. If hard drive space is at a premium and you don't plan on doing major system updates, you can get by with as little as 30 or 40 MB.

- `/tmp`: temporary data created by programs will most likely go in this directory. 40–100MB should usually be enough. Some applications — including archive manipulators, CD/DVD authoring tools, and multimedia software — may use `/tmp` to temporarily store image files. If you plan to use such applications, you should adjust the space available in `/tmp` accordingly.

- `/home`: every user will put his personal data into a subdirectory of this directory. Its size depends on how many users will be using the system and what files are to be stored in their directories. Depending on your planned usage you should reserve about 100MB for each user, but adapt this value to your needs. Reserve a lot more space if you plan to save a lot of multimedia files (pictures, MP3, movies) in your home directory.

C.3. Recommended Partitioning Scheme

For new users, personal Ubuntu boxes, home systems, and other single-user setups, a single / partition (plus swap) is probably the easiest, simplest way to go. However, if your partition is larger than around 6GB, choose ext3 as your partition type. Ext2 partitions need periodic file system integrity checking, and this can cause delays during booting when the partition is large.

For multi-user systems or systems with lots of disk space, it's best to put `/usr`, `/var`, `/tmp`, and `/home` each on their own partitions separate from the / partition.

You might need a separate `/usr/local` partition if you plan to install many programs that are not part of the Ubuntu distribution. If your machine will be a mail server, you might need to make `/var/mail` a separate partition. Often, putting `/tmp` on its own partition, for

143

instance 20–50MB, is a good idea. If you are setting up a server with lots of user accounts, it's generally good to have a separate, large /home partition. In general, the partitioning situation varies from computer to computer depending on its uses.

For very complex systems, you should see the *Multi Disk HOWTO*[2]. This contains in-depth information, mostly of interest to ISPs and people setting up servers.

With respect to the issue of swap partition size, there are many views. One rule of thumb which works well is to use as much swap as you have system memory. It also shouldn't be smaller than 16MB, in most cases. Of course, there are exceptions to these rules. If you are trying to solve 10000 simultaneous equations on a machine with 256MB of memory, you may need a gigabyte (or more) of swap.

On 32-bit architectures (i386, m68k, 32-bit SPARC, and PowerPC), the maximum size of a swap partition is 2GB. That should be enough for nearly any installation. However, if your swap requirements are this high, you should probably try to spread the swap across different disks (also called "spindles") and, if possible, different SCSI or IDE channels. The kernel will balance swap usage between multiple swap partitions, giving better performance.

As an example, an older home machine might have 32MB of RAM and a 1.7GB IDE drive on /dev/hda. There might be a 500MB partition for another operating system on /dev/hda1, a 32MB swap partition on /dev/hda3 and about 1.2GB on /dev/hda2 as the Linux partition.

For an idea of the space required by Ubuntu, check *the section called "Disk Space Needed"*.

C.4. Device Names in Linux

Linux disks and partition names may be different from other operating systems. You need to know the names that Linux uses when you create and mount partitions. Here's the basic naming scheme:

- The first floppy drive is named /dev/fd0 .
- The second floppy drive is named /dev/fd1 .
- The first SCSI disk (SCSI ID address-wise) is named /dev/sda.
- The second SCSI disk (address-wise) is named /dev/sdb, and so on.
- The first SCSI CD-ROM is named /dev/scd0 , also known as /dev/sr0.
- The master disk on IDE primary controller is named /dev/hda.
- The slave disk on IDE primary controller is named /dev/hdb.

---

[2] *http://www.tldp.org/HOWTO/Multi-Disk-HOWTO.html*

- The master and slave disks of the secondary controller can be called /dev/hdc and /dev/hdd, respectively. Newer IDE controllers can actually have two channels, effectively acting like two controllers.

The partitions on each disk are represented by appending a decimal number to the disk name: sda1 and sda2 represent the first and second partitions of the first SCSI disk drive in your system.

Here is a real-life example. Let's assume you have a system with 2 SCSI disks, one at SCSI address 2 and the other at SCSI address 4. The first disk (at address 2) is then named sda, and the second sdb. If the sda drive has 3 partitions on it, these will be named sda1, sda2, and sda3. The same applies to the sdb disk and its partitions.

Note that if you have two SCSI host bus adapters (i.e., controllers), the order of the drives can get confusing. The best solution in this case is to watch the boot messages, assuming you know the drive models and/or capacities.

Linux represents the primary partitions as the drive name, plus the numbers 1 through 4. For example, the first primary partition on the first IDE drive is /dev/hda1. The logical partitions are numbered starting at 5, so the first logical partition on that same drive is /dev/hda5. Remember that the extended partition, that is, the primary partition holding the logical partitions, is not usable by itself. This applies to SCSI disks as well as IDE disks.

C.5. Ubuntu Partitioning Programs

Several varieties of partitioning programs have been adapted by Debian and Ubuntu developers to work on various types of hard disks and computer architectures. Following is a list of the program(s) applicable for your architecture.

partman

Recommended partitioning tool in Ubuntu. This Swiss army knife can also resize partitions, create filesystems ("format" in Windows speak) and assign them to the mountpoints.

fdisk

The original Linux disk partitioner, good for gurus.

Be careful if you have existing FreeBSD partitions on your machine. The installation kernels include support for these partitions, but the way that **fdisk** represents them (or not) can make the device names differ. See the *Linux+FreeBSD HOWTO*[3].

---

[3] http://www.tldp.org/HOWTO/Linux+FreeBSD-2.html

cfdisk

> A simple-to-use, full-screen disk partitioner for the rest of us.
>
> Note that **cfdisk** doesn't understand FreeBSD partitions at all, and, again, device names may differ as a result.

One of these programs will be run by default when you select Partition disks (or similar). It may be possible to use a different partitioning tool from the command line on VT2, but this is not recommended.

Remember to mark your boot partition as "Bootable".

C.5.1. Partitioning for Intel x86

If you have an existing other operating system such as DOS or Windows and you want to preserve that operating system while installing Ubuntu, you may need to resize its partition to free up space for the Ubuntu installation. The installer supports resizing of both FAT and NTFS filesystems; when you get to the installer's partitioning step, select the option Manual and then simply select an existing partition and change its size.

The PC BIOS generally adds additional constraints for disk partitioning. There is a limit to how many "primary" and "logical" partitions a drive can contain. Additionally, with pre 1994–98 BIOSes, there are limits to where on the drive the BIOS can boot from. More information can be found in the *Linux Partition HOWTO*[4] and the *Phoenix BIOS FAQ*[5], but this section will include a brief overview to help you plan most situations.

"Primary" partitions are the original partitioning scheme for PC disks. However, there can only be four of them. To get past this limitation, "extended" and "logical" partitions were invented. By setting one of your primary partitions as an extended partition, you can subdivide all the space allocated to that partition into logical partitions. You can create up to 60 logical partitions per extended partition; however, you can only have one extended partition per drive.

Linux limits the partitions per drive to 15 partitions for SCSI disks (3 usable primary partitions, 12 logical partitions), and 63 partitions on an IDE drive (3 usable primary partitions, 60 logical partitions). However the normal Ubuntu system provides only 20 devices for partitions, so you may not install on partitions higher than 20 unless you first manually create devices for those partitions.

If you have a large IDE disk, and are using neither LBA addressing, nor overlay drivers (sometimes provided by hard disk manufacturers), then the boot partition (the partition

---

[4] *http://www.tldp.org/HOWTO/Partition/*
[5] *http://www.phoenix.com/en/Customer+Services/BIOS/BIOS+FAQ/default.htm*

containing your kernel image) must be placed within the first 1024 cylinders of your hard drive (usually around 524 megabytes, without BIOS translation).

This restriction doesn't apply if you have a BIOS newer than around 1995-98 (depending on the manufacturer) that supports the "Enhanced Disk Drive Support Specification". Both Lilo, the Linux loader, and Ubuntu's alternative **mbr** must use the BIOS to read the kernel from the disk into RAM. If the BIOS int 0x13 large disk access extensions are found to be present, they will be utilized. Otherwise, the legacy disk access interface is used as a fall-back, and it cannot be used to address any location on the disk higher than the 1023rd cylinder. Once Linux is booted, no matter what BIOS your computer has, these restrictions no longer apply, since Linux does not use the BIOS for disk access.

If you have a large disk, you might have to use cylinder translation techniques, which you can set from your BIOS setup program, such as LBA (Logical Block Addressing) or CHS translation mode ("Large"). More information about issues with large disks can be found in the *Large Disk HOWTO*[6]. If you are using a cylinder translation scheme, and the BIOS does not support the large disk access extensions, then your boot partition has to fit within the *translated* representation of the 1024th cylinder.

The recommended way of accomplishing this is to create a small (25-50MB should suffice) partition at the beginning of the disk to be used as the boot partition, and then create whatever other partitions you wish to have, in the remaining area. This boot partition *must* be mounted on /boot, since that is the directory where the Linux kernel(s) will be stored. This configuration will work on any system, regardless of whether LBA or large disk CHS translation is used, and regardless of whether your BIOS supports the large disk access extensions.

---

[6] http://www.tldp.org/HOWTO/Large-Disk-HOWTO.html

Appendix D.
Random Bits

D.1. Linux Devices

In Linux various special files can be found under the directory /dev. These files are called device files and behave unlike ordinary files. The most common types of device files are for block devices and character devices. These files are an interface to the actual driver (part of the Linux kernel) which in turn accesses the hardware. Another, less common, type of device file is the named *pipe*. The most important device files are listed in the tables below.

fd0	First Floppy Drive
fd1	Second Floppy Drive

hda	IDE Hard disk / CD-ROM on the first IDE port (Master)
hdb	IDE Hard disk / CD-ROM on the first IDE port (Slave)
hdc	IDE Hard disk / CD-ROM on the second IDE port (Master)
hdd	IDE Hard disk / CD-ROM on the second IDE port (Slave)
hda1	First partition of the first IDE hard disk
hdd15	Fifteenth partition of the fourth IDE hard disk

sda	SCSI Hard disk with lowest SCSI ID (e.g. 0)
sdb	SCSI Hard disk with next higher SCSI ID (e.g. 1)
sdc	SCSI Hard disk with next higher SCSI ID (e.g. 2)
sda1	First partition of the first SCSI hard disk
sdd10	Tenth partition of the fourth SCSI hard disk

sr0	SCSI CD-ROM with the lowest SCSI ID
sr1	SCSI CD-ROM with the next higher SCSI ID

Installation Guide

ttyS0	Serial port 0, COM1 under MS-DOS
ttyS1	Serial port 1, COM2 under MS-DOS
psaux	PS/2 mouse device
gpmdata	Pseudo device, repeater data from GPM (mouse) daemon

cdrom	Symbolic link to the CD-ROM drive
mouse	Symbolic link to the mouse device file

null	Anything written to this device will disappear
zero	One can endlessly read zeros out of this device

D.1.1. Setting Up Your Mouse

The mouse can be used in both the Linux console (with gpm) and the X window environment. Normally, this is a simple matter of installing gpm and the X server itself. Both should be configured to use /dev/input/mice as the mouse device. The correct mouse protocol is named **exps2** in gpm, and **ExplorerPS/2** in X. The respective configuration files are /etc/gpm.conf and /etc/X11/xorg.conf.

Certain kernel modules must be loaded in order for your mouse to work. In most cases the correct modules are autodetected, but not always for old-style serial and bus mice[1], which are quite rare except on very old computers. Summary of Linux kernel modules needed for different mouse types:

Module	Description
psmouse	PS/2 mice (should be autodetected)
usbhid	USB mice (should be autodetected)
sermouse	Most serial mice
logibm	Bus mouse connected to Logitech adapter card
inport	Bus mouse connected to ATI or Microsoft InPort card

To load a mouse driver module, you can use the **modconf** command (from the package with the same name) and look in the category `kernel/drivers/input/mouse`.

---

[1] Serial mice usually have a 9-hole D-shaped connector; bus mice have an 8-pin round connector, not to be confused with the 6-pin round connector of a PS/2 mouse or the 4-pin round connector of an ADB mouse.

Ubuntu 9.10

D.2. Disk Space Needed for Tasks

A standard installation for the i386 architecture, including all standard packages and using the default 2.6 kernel, takes up 397MB of disk space. A minimal base installation, without the "Standard system" task selected, will take 250MB.

> **Important**
>
> In both cases this is the actual disk space used *after* the installation is finished and any temporary files deleted. It also does not take into account overhead used by the file system, for example for journal files. This means that significantly more disk space is needed both *during* the installation and for normal system use.

The following table lists sizes reported by aptitude for the tasks listed in tasksel. Note that some tasks have overlapping constituents, so the total installed size for two tasks together may be less than the total obtained by adding up the numbers.

Note that you will need to add the sizes listed in the table to the size of the standard installation when determining the size of partitions. Most of the size listed as "Installed size" will end up in /usr and in /lib; the size listed as "Download size" is (temporarily) required in /var.

Task	Installed size (MB)	Download size (MB)	Space needed to install (MB)
Desktop environment	1830	703	2533
Laptop[a]	26	9	35
Web server	42	13	55
Print server	215	84	299
DNS server	3	1	4
File server	74	29	103
Mail server	14	5	19
SQL database	50	18	68
[a] There is some overlap of the Laptop task with the Desktop environment task. If you install both, the Laptop task will only require a few MB additional disk space.			

> **Note**
>
> The *Desktop* task will install the GNOME desktop environment.

If you install in a language other than English, **tasksel** may automatically install a *localization task*, if one is available for your language. Space requirements differ per language; you should allow up to 350MB in total for download and installation.

Installation Guide

D.3. Disk Space Needed

A minimal server installation of jaunty requires 400MB of disk space. The standard Ubuntu desktop installation requires 2GB.

D.4. Installing Ubuntu from a Unix/Linux System

This section explains how to install Ubuntu from an existing Unix or Linux system, without using the menu-driven installer as explained in the rest of the manual. This "cross-install" HOWTO has been requested by users switching to Ubuntu from Debian GNU/Linux, Red Hat, Mandrake, and SUSE. In this section some familiarity with entering *nix commands and navigating the file system is assumed. In this section, $ symbolizes a command to be entered in the user's current system, while # refers to a command entered in the Ubuntu chroot.

Once you've got the new Ubuntu system configured to your preference, you can migrate your existing user data (if any) to it, and keep on rolling. This is therefore a "zero downtime" Ubuntu install. It's also a clever way for dealing with hardware that otherwise doesn't play friendly with various boot or installation media.

> **Note**
>
> As this is a mostly manual procedure, you should bear in mind that you will need to do a lot of basic configuration of the system yourself, which will also require more knowledge of Ubuntu and of Linux in general than performing a regular installation. You cannot expect this procedure to result in a system that is identical to a system from a regular installation. You should also keep in mind that this procedure only gives the basic steps to set up a system. Additional installation and/or configuration steps may be needed.

D.4.1. Getting Started

With your current *nix partitioning tools, repartition the hard drive as needed, creating at least one filesystem plus swap. You need around 350MB of space available for a console only install, or about 1GB if you plan to install X (more if you intend to install desktop environments like GNOME or KDE).

Next, create file systems on the partitions. For example, to create an ext3 file system on partition /dev/hda6 (that's our example root partition):

```
# mke2fs -j /dev/hda6
```

To create an ext2 file system instead, omit -j.

Initialize and activate swap (substitute the partition number for your intended Ubuntu swap partition):

Ubuntu 9.10

```
# mkswap /dev/hda5
# sync; sync; sync
# swapon /dev/hda5
```

Mount one partition as /mnt/ubuntu (the installation point, to be the root (/) filesystem on your new system). The mount point name is strictly arbitrary, it is referenced later below.

```
# mkdir /mnt/ubuntu
# mount /dev/hda6 /mnt/ubuntu
```

> **Note**
>
> If you want to have parts of the filesystem (e.g. /usr) mounted on separate partitions, you will need to create and mount these directories manually before proceding with the next stage.

D.4.2. Install debootstrap

The utility used by the Ubuntu installer, and recognized as the official way to install an Ubuntu base system, is **debootstrap**. It uses **wget** and **ar**, but otherwise depends only on /bin/sh and basic Unix/Linux tools[2]. Install **wget** and **ar** if they aren't already on your current system, then download and install **debootstrap**.

Or, you can use the following procedure to install it manually. Make a work folder for extracting the .deb into:

```
# mkdir work
# cd work
```

The **debootstrap** binary is located in the Ubuntu archive (be sure to select the proper file for your architecture). Download the **debootstrap** .deb from the *pool*[3], copy the package to the work folder, and extract the files from it. You will need to have root privileges to install the files.

```
# ar -x debootstrap_0.X.X_all.deb
# cd /
# zcat /full-path-to-work/work/data.tar.gz | tar xv
```

D.4.3. Run debootstrap

debootstrap can download the needed files directly from the archive when you run it. You can substitute any Ubuntu archive mirror for **archive.ubuntu.com/ubuntu** in the command example below, preferably a mirror close to you network-wise. Mirrors are listed at *http://wiki.ubuntu.com/Archive*.

---

[2] These include the GNU core utilities and commands like **sed**, **grep**, **tar** and **gzip**.
[3] *http://archive.ubuntu.com/ubuntu/pool/main/d/debootstrap/*

Installation Guide

If you have an Ubuntu jaunty CD mounted at /cdrom, you could substitute a file URL instead of the http URL: `file:/cdrom/ubuntu/`

Substitute one of the following for ARCH in the **debootstrap** command: `amd64`, `armel`, `hppa`, `i386`, `ia64`, `powerpc`, or `sparc`.

```
# /usr/sbin/debootstrap --arch ARCH jaunty /mnt/ubuntu
```

D.4.4. Configure The Base System

Now you've got a real Ubuntu system, though rather lean, on disk. **Chroot** into it:

```
# LANG=C chroot /mnt/ubuntu /bin/bash
```

After chrooting you may need to set the terminal definition to be compatible with the Ubuntu base system, for example:

```
# export TERM=xterm-color
```

D.4.4.1. Create device files

At this point /dev/ only contains very basic device files. For the next steps of the installation additional device files may be needed. There are different ways to go about this and which method you should use depends on the host system you are using for the installation, on whether you intend to use a modular kernel or not, and on whether you intend to use dynamic (e.g. using udev) or static device files for the new system.

A few of the available options are:

- create a default set of static device files using
  ```
  # cd /dev
  # MAKEDEV generic
  ```
- manually create only specific device files using **MAKEDEV**
- bind mount /dev from your host system on top of /dev in the target system; note that the postinst scripts of some packages may try to create device files, so this option should only be used with care

D.4.4.2. Mount Partitions

You need to create /etc/fstab.

```
# editor /etc/fstab
```

Here is a sample you can modify to suit:

```
# /etc/fstab: static file system information.
#
# file system     mount point    type    options     dump pass
/dev/XXX             /           ext3    defaults      0    1
```

153

Ubuntu 9.10

/dev/XXX	/boot	ext3	ro,nosuid,nodev	0	2
/dev/XXX	none	swap	sw	0	0
proc	/proc	proc	defaults	0	0
sys	/sys	sysfs	defaults	0	0
/dev/fd0	/media/floppy	auto	noauto,rw,sync,user,exec	0	0
/dev/cdrom	/media/cdrom	iso9660	noauto,ro,user,exec	0	0
/dev/XXX	/tmp	ext3	rw,nosuid,nodev	0	2
/dev/XXX	/var	ext3	rw,nosuid,nodev	0	2
/dev/XXX	/usr	ext3	rw,nodev	0	2
/dev/XXX	/home	ext3	rw,nosuid,nodev	0	2

Use **mount -a** to mount all the file systems you have specified in your /etc/fstab, or, to mount file systems individually, use:

```
# mount /path    # e.g.: mount /usr
```

Current Ubuntu systems have mountpoints for removable media under /media, but keep compatibility symlinks in /. Create these as as needed, for example:

```
# cd /media
# mkdir cdrom0
# ln -s cdrom0 cdrom
# cd /
# ln -s media/cdrom
```

You can mount the proc and sysfs file systems multiple times and to arbitrary locations, though /proc and /sys respectively are customary. If you didn't use **mount -a**, be sure to mount proc and sysfs before continuing:

```
# mount -t proc proc /proc
# mount -t sysfs sysfs /sys
```

The command **ls /proc** should now show a non-empty directory. Should this fail, you may be able to mount proc from outside the chroot:

```
# mount -t proc proc /mnt/ubuntu/proc
```

D.4.4.3. Setting Timezone

An option in the file /etc/default/rcS determines whether the system will interpret the hardware clock as being set to UTC or local time. The following command allow you to set that and choose your timezone.

```
# editor /etc/default/rcS
# tzconfig
```

D.4.4.4. Configure Networking

To configure networking, edit /etc/network/interfaces, /etc/resolv.conf, /etc/hostname and /etc/hosts.

Installation Guide

```
# editor /etc/network/interfaces
```

Here are some simple examples from /usr/share/doc/ifupdown/examples:

```
######################################################################
# /etc/network/interfaces -- configuration file for ifup(8), ifdown(8)
# See the interfaces(5) manpage for information on what options are
# available.
######################################################################

# We always want the loopback interface.
#
auto lo
iface lo inet loopback

# To use dhcp:
#
# auto eth0
# iface eth0 inet dhcp

# An example static IP setup: (broadcast and gateway are optional)
#
# auto eth0
# iface eth0 inet static
#     address 192.168.0.42
#     network 192.168.0.0
#     netmask 255.255.255.0
#     broadcast 192.168.0.255
#     gateway 192.168.0.1
```

Enter your nameserver(s) and search directives in /etc/resolv.conf:

```
# editor /etc/resolv.conf
```

A simple example /etc/resolv.conf:

```
search hqdom.local
nameserver 10.1.1.36
nameserver 192.168.9.100
```

Enter your system's host name (2 to 63 characters):

```
# echo UbuntuHostName > /etc/hostname
```

And a basic /etc/hosts with IPv6 support:

```
127.0.0.1 localhost UbuntuHostName

# The following lines are desirable for IPv6 capable hosts
::1     ip6-localhost ip6-loopback
fe00::0 ip6-localnet
ff00::0 ip6-mcastprefix
ff02::1 ip6-allnodes
ff02::2 ip6-allrouters
ff02::3 ip6-allhosts
```

Ubuntu 9.10

If you have multiple network cards, you should arrange the names of driver modules in the /etc/modules file into the desired order. Then during boot, each card will be associated with the interface name (eth0, eth1, etc.) that you expect.

D.4.4.5. Configure Apt

Debootstrap will have created a very basic /etc/apt/sources.list that will allow installing additional packages. However, you may want to add some additional sources, for example for source packages and security updates:

```
deb-src http://archive.ubuntu.com/ubuntu jaunty main

deb http://security.ubuntu.com/ubuntu jaunty-security main
deb-src http://security.ubuntu.com/ubuntu jaunty-security main
```

Make sure to run **aptitude update** after you have made changes to the sources list.

D.4.4.6. Configure Locales and Keyboard

To configure your locale settings to use a language other than English, install the appropriate language packs and configure them. Currently the use of UTF-8 locales is recommended.

```
# aptitude install language-pack-de language-pack-gnome-de
```

To configure your keyboard (if needed):

```
# aptitude install console-setup
# dpkg-reconfigure console-setup
```

Note that the keyboard cannot be set while in the chroot, but will be configured for the next reboot.

D.4.5. Install a Kernel

If you intend to boot this system, you probably want a Linux kernel and a boot loader. Identify available pre-packaged kernels with:

```
# apt-cache search linux-image
```

If you intend to use a pre-packaged kernel, you may want to create the configuration file /etc/kernel-img.conf before you do so. Here's an example file:

```
# Kernel image management overrides
# See kernel-img.conf(5) for details
do_symlinks = yes
relative_links = yes
do_bootloader = yes
do_bootfloppy = no
do_initrd = yes
link_in_boot = no
```

For detailed information about this file and the various options, consult its man page which will be available after installing the `kernel-package` package. We recommend that you check that the values are appropriate for your system.

Then install the kernel package of your choice using its package name.

```
# aptitude install linux-image-2.6.28-arch-etc
```

If you did not create a `/etc/kernel-img.conf` before installing a pre-packaged kernel, you may be asked some questions during its installation that refer to it.

D.4.6. Set up the Boot Loader

To make your Ubuntu system bootable, set up your boot loader to load the installed kernel with your new root partition. Note that **debootstrap** does not install a boot loader, though you can use **aptitude** inside your Ubuntu chroot to do so.

Check `info grub` or `man lilo.conf` for instructions on setting up the bootloader. For an initial install of grub, you should normally run **grub-install** to install a grub image on your hard disk, and **update-grub** to generate a `menu.lst` configuration file. If you are keeping the system you used to install Ubuntu, just add an entry for the Ubuntu install to your existing grub `menu.lst` or `lilo.conf`. For `lilo.conf`, you could also copy it to the new system and edit it there. After you are done editing, call **lilo** (remember it will use `lilo.conf` relative to the system you call it from).

Installing and setting up `grub` is as easy as:

```
# aptitude install grub
# grub-install /dev/hda
# update-grub
```

The second command will install **grub** (in this case in the MBR of `hda`). The last command will create a sane and working `/boot/grub/menu.lst`.

Note that this assumes that a `/dev/hda` device file has been created. There are alternative methods to install **grub**, but those are outside the scope of this appendix.

Here is a basic `/etc/lilo.conf` as an example:

```
boot=/dev/hda6
root=/dev/hda6
install=menu
delay=20
lba32
image=/vmlinuz
initrd=/initrd.img
label=Ubuntu
```

Depending on which bootloader you selected, you can now make some additional changes in `/etc/kernel-img.conf`.

For the `grub` bootloader, you should set the `do_bootloader` option to "no". And to automatically update your `/boot/grub/menu.lst` on installation or removal of Ubuntu kernels, add the following lines:

```
postinst_hook = update-grub
postrm_hook   = update-grub
```

For the `lilo` bootloader, the value of `do_bootloader` needs to remain "yes".

D.4.7. Finishing touches

As mentioned earlier, the installed system will be very basic. If you would like to make the system a bit more mature, there is an easy method to install all packages with "standard" priority:

```
# tasksel install standard
```

Of course, you can also just use **aptitude** to install packages individually.

After the installation there will be a lot of downloaded packages in `/var/cache/apt/archives/`. You can free up some diskspace by running:

```
# aptitude clean
```

D.4.8. Create a User

Use the **adduser** command to create a new user account:

```
# adduser myusername
```

You will be prompted for a full name and a password.

The normal Ubuntu configuration is to allow this new user to administer the system using **sudo**. To set this up, first create an `admin` group and add your new user to it:

```
# addgroup --system admin
# adduser myusername admin
```

You can now use the **visudo** command to add these lines to the end of `/etc/sudoers`, so that any user in the `admin` group can administer the system:

```
# Members of the admin group may gain root privileges
%admin ALL=(ALL) ALL
```

If you don't want to follow this configuration, then remember to set a root **password**:

```
# passwd root
```

D.4.9. Install the Ubuntu Desktop

At this point, you probably want to reboot into your new Ubuntu system to make sure it all works. Once you've done that, log in as the user you just created, and run:

```
$ sudo tasksel install standard
$ sudo tasksel install ubuntu-desktop
```

You will need to enter your password to authorise **sudo** to run as root.

tasksel will now get on with installing the packages that make up the Ubuntu desktop, which will take a while. When it's finished, you should be presented with a graphical login prompt. The installation is now complete, so go ahead and log in.

D.5. Installing Ubuntu over Parallel Line IP (PLIP)

This section explains how to install Ubuntu on a computer without an Ethernet card, but with just a remote gateway computer attached via a Null-Modem cable (also called Null-Printer cable). The gateway computer should be connected to a network that has an Ubuntu mirror on it (e.g. to the Internet).

In the example in this appendix we will set up a PLIP connection using a gateway connected to the Internet over a dial-up connection (ppp0). We will use IP addresses 192.168.0.1 and 192.168.0.2 for the PLIP interfaces on the target system and the source system respectively (these addresses should be unused within your network address space).

The PLIP connection set up during the installation will also be available after the reboot into the installed system (see *Chapter 7, Booting Into Your New Ubuntu System*).

Before you start, you will need to check the BIOS configuration (IO base address and IRQ) for the parallel ports of both the source and target systems. The most common values are `io=0x378`, `irq=7`.

D.5.1. Requirements

- A target computer, called *target*, where Ubuntu will be installed.
- System installation media; see *the section called "Installation Media"*.
- Another computer connected to the Internet, called *source*, that will function as the gateway.
- A DB-25 Null-Modem cable. See the *PLIP-Install-HOWTO*[4] for more information on this cable and instructions how to make your own.

D.5.2. Setting up source

The following shell script is a simple example of how to configure the source computer as a gateway to the Internet using ppp0.

---

[4] *http://www.tldp.org/HOWTO/PLIP-Install-HOWTO.html*

```sh
#!/bin/sh

# We remove running modules from kernel to avoid conflicts and to
# reconfigure them manually.
modprobe -r lp parport_pc
modprobe parport_pc io=0x378 irq=7
modprobe plip

# Configure the plip interface (plip0 for me, see dmesg | grep plip)
ifconfig plip0 192.168.0.2 pointopoint 192.168.0.1 netmask 255.255.255.255 up

# Configure gateway
modprobe iptable_nat
iptables -t nat -A POSTROUTING -o ppp0 -j MASQUERADE
echo 1 > /proc/sys/net/ipv4/ip_forward
```

D.5.3. Installing target

Boot the installation media. The installation needs to be run in expert mode; enter **expert** at the boot prompt. If you need to set parameters for kernel modules, you also need to do this at the boot prompt. For example, to boot the installer and set values for the "io" and "irq" options for the parport_pc module, enter the following at the boot prompt:

```
expert parport_pc.io=0x378 parport_pc.irq=7
```

Below are the answers that should be given during various stages of the installation.

1. Load installer components from CD

    Select the **plip-modules** option from the list; this will make the PLIP drivers available to the installation system.

2. Detect network hardware

    - If target *does* have a network card, a list of driver modules for detected cards will be shown. If you want to force debian-installer to use plip instead, you have to deselect all listed driver modules. Obviously, if target doesn't have a network card, the installer will not show this list.
    - Because no network card was detected/selected earlier, the installer will ask you to select a network driver module from a list. Select the **plip** module.

3. Configure the network

    - Auto-configure network with DHCP: No
    - IP address: *192.168.0.1*
    - Point-to-point address: *192.168.0.2*
    - Name server addresses: you can enter the same addresses used on source (see /etc/resolv.conf)

Installation Guide

D.6. Installing Ubuntu using PPP over Ethernet (PPPoE)

In some countries PPP over Ethernet (PPPoE) is a common protocol for broadband (ADSL or cable) connections to an Internet Service Provider. Setting up a network connection using PPPoE is not supported by default in the installer, but can be made to work very simply. This section explains how.

The PPPoE connection set up during the installation will also be available after the reboot into the installed system (see *Chapter 7, Booting Into Your New Ubuntu System*).

To have the option of setting up and using PPPoE during the installation, you will need to install using one of the CD-ROM/DVD images that are available. It is not supported for other installation methods (e.g. netboot).

Installing over PPPoE is mostly the same as any other installation. The following steps explain the differences.

- Boot the installer with `modules=ppp-udeb` as boot parameter. This means that at the boot prompt you should enter:

  ```
  install modules=ppp-udeb
  ```

  or, if you prefer using the graphical installer:

  ```
  installgui modules=ppp-udeb
  ```

  This will ensure the component responsible for the setup of PPPoE (`ppp-udeb`) will be loaded and run automatically.

- Follow the regular initial steps of the installation (language, country and keyboard selection; the loading of additional installer components[5]).

- The next step is the detection of network hardware, in order to identify any Ethernet cards present in the system.

- After this the actual setup of PPPoE is started. The installer will probe all the detected Ethernet interfaces in an attempt to find a PPPoE concentrator (a type of server which handles PPPoE connections).

  It is possible that the concentrator will not to be found at the first attempt. This can happen occasionally on slow or loaded networks or with faulty servers. In most cases a second attempt to detect the concentrator will be successful; to retry, select Configure and start a PPPoE connection from the main menu of the installer.

---

[5] The `ppp-udeb` component is loaded as one of the additional components in this step. If you want to install at medium or low priority (expert mode), you can also manually select the `ppp-udeb` instead of entering the "modules" parameter at the boot prompt.

- After a concentrator is found, the user will be prompted to type the login information (the PPPoE username and password).
- At this point the installer will use the provided information to establish the PPPoE connection. If the correct information was provided, the PPPoE connection should be configured and the installer should be able to use it to connect to the Internet and retrieve packages over it (if needed). If the login information is not correct or some error appears, the installer will stop, but the configuration can be attempted again by selecting the menu entry Configure and start a PPPoE connection.

D.7. The Graphical Installer

The graphical version of the installer is only available for a limited number of architectures, including Intel x86. The functionality of the graphical installer is essentially the same as that of the regular installer as it basically uses the same programs, but with a different frontend.

Although the functionality is identical, the graphical installer still has a few significant advantages. The main advantage is that it supports more languages, namely those that use a character set that cannot be displayed with the regular "newt" frontend. It also has a few usability advantages such as the option to use a mouse, and in some cases several questions can be displayed on a single screen.

The graphical installer is available with all CD images and with the hd-media installation method. To boot the graphical installer simply select the relevant option from the boot menu. Expert and rescue mode for the graphical installer can be selected from the "Advanced options" menu. The previously used boot methods **installgui**, **expertgui** and **rescuegui** can still be used from the boot prompt which is shown after selecting the "Help" option in the boot menu.

There is also a graphical installer image that can be netbooted. And there is a special "mini" ISO image[6], which is mainly useful for testing.

Just as with the regular installer it is possible to add boot parameters when starting the graphical installer. One of those parameters allows to configure the mouse for left-handed use. Others allow to select the mouse device (e.g. for a serial mouse) and the mouse protocol. See *the section called "Boot Parameters"* for valid parameters and *the section called "The Boot Screen"* for information on how to pass them.

---

[6] The mini ISO image can be downloaded from a Debian mirror as described in *the section called "Downloading Files from Ubuntu Mirrors"*. Look for `netboot/gtk/mini.iso`.

> **Note**
>
> The graphical installer requires significantly more memory to run than the regular installer: 96MB. If insufficient memory is available, it will automatically fall back to the regular "newt" frontend.
>
> If the amount of memory in your system is below 44MB, the graphical installer may fail to boot at all while booting the regular installer would still work. Using the regular installer is recommended for systems with little available memory.

D.7.1. Using the graphical installer

As already mentioned, the graphical installer basically works the same as the regular installer and thus the rest of this manual can be used to guide you through the installation process.

If you prefer using the keyboard over the mouse, there are two things you need to know. To expand a collapsed list (used for example for the selection of countries within continents), you can use the **+** and **-** keys. For questions where more than one item can be selected (e.g. task selection), you first need to tab to the **Continue** button after making your selections; hitting enter will toggle a selection, not activate **Continue**.

To switch to another console, you will also need to use the **Ctrl** key, just as with the X Window System. For example, to switch to VT2 (the first debug shell) you would use: **Ctrl+ Left Alt+ F2**. The graphical installer itself runs on VT5, so you can use **Left Alt+ F5** to switch back.

D.7.2. Known issues

The graphical frontend to the installer is relatively new and because of that there are some known issues. We continue to work on resolving these.

- Information on some screens is not yet nicely formatted into columns as it should be.
- Support for touchpads is not yet optimal.

Appendix E.
Administrivia

E.1. About This Document

This manual was created for Sarge's debian-installer, based on the Woody installation manual for boot-floppies, which was based on earlier Debian installation manuals, and on the Progeny distribution manual which was released under GPL in 2003. It was subsequently modified for use in Ubuntu.

This document is written in DocBook XML. Output formats are generated by various programs using information from the `docbook-xml` and `docbook-xsl` packages.

In order to increase the maintainability of this document, we use a number of XML features, such as entities and profiling attributes. These play a role akin to variables and conditionals in programming languages. The XML source to this document contains information for each different architecture — profiling attributes are used to isolate certain bits of text as architecture-specific.

E.2. Contributing to This Document

If you have problems or suggestions regarding this document, please mail them to `<ubuntu-users@lists.ubuntu.com>`.

Please do *not* contact the authors of this document directly. There is also a discussion list for `debian-installer`, which includes discussions of this manual. The mailing list is `<debian-boot@lists.debian.org>`. Instructions for subscribing to this list can be found at the *Debian Mailing List Subscription*[1] page; or you can browse the *Debian Mailing List Archives*[2] online. Please do not contact debian-boot about issues specific to Ubuntu.

---

[1] *http://www.debian.org/MailingLists/subscribe*
[2] *http://lists.debian.org/*

E.3. Major Contributions

This document was originally written by Bruce Perens, Sven Rudolph, Igor Grobman, James Treacy, and Adam Di Carlo. Sebastian Ley wrote the Installation Howto. Many, many Debian users and developers contributed to this document. Particular note must be made of Michael Schmitz (m68k support), Frank Neumann (original author of the *Amiga install manual*[3]), Arto Astala, Eric Delaunay/Ben Collins (SPARC information), Tapio Lehtonen, and Stéphane Bortzmeyer for numerous edits and text. We have to thank Pascal Le Bail for useful information about booting from USB memory sticks. Miroslav Kuře has documented a lot of the new functionality in Sarge's debian-installer. Colin Watson made the modifications for Ubuntu.

Extremely helpful text and information was found in Jim Mintha's HOWTO for network booting (no URL available), the *Debian FAQ*[4], the *Linux/m68k FAQ*[5], the *Linux for SPARC Processors FAQ*[6], the *Linux/Alpha FAQ*[7], amongst others. The maintainers of these freely available and rich sources of information must be recognized.

The section on chrooted installations in this manual (*the section called "Installing Ubuntu from a Unix/Linux System"*) was derived in part from documents copyright Karsten M. Self.

The section on installations over plip in this manual (*the section called "Installing Ubuntu over Parallel Line IP (PLIP)"*) was based on the *PLIP-Install-HOWTO*[8] by Gilles Lamiral.

E.4. Trademark Acknowledgement

All trademarks are property of their respective trademark owners.

---

[3] *http://www.informatik.uni-oldenburg.de/~amigo/debian_inst.html*
[4] *http://www.debian.org/doc/FAQ/*
[5] *http://www.linux-m68k.org/faq/faq.html*
[6] *http://www.ultralinux.org/faq.html*
[7] *http://linux.iol.unh.edu/linux/alpha/faq/*
[8] *http://www.tldp.org/HOWTO/PLIP-Install-HOWTO.html*

Appendix F.
GNU General Public License

Version 2, June 1991

```
Copyright (C) 1989, 1991 Free Software Foundation, Inc.
51 Franklin St, Fifth Floor, Boston, MA 02110-1301, USA.

Everyone is permitted to copy and distribute verbatim copies
of this license document, but changing it is not allowed.
```

F.1. Preamble

The licenses for most software are designed to take away your freedom to share and change it. By contrast, the gnu General Public License is intended to guarantee your freedom to share and change free software — to make sure the software is free for all its users. This General Public License applies to most of the Free Software Foundation's software and to any other program whose authors commit to using it. (Some other Free Software Foundation software is covered by the gnu Library General Public License instead.) You can apply it to your programs, too.

When we speak of free software, we are referring to freedom, not price. Our General Public Licenses are designed to make sure that you have the freedom to distribute copies of free software (and charge for this service if you wish), that you receive source code or can get it if you want it, that you can change the software or use pieces of it in new free programs; and that you know you can do these things.

To protect your rights, we need to make restrictions that forbid anyone to deny you these rights or to ask you to surrender the rights. These restrictions translate to certain responsibilities for you if you distribute copies of the software, or if you modify it.

For example, if you distribute copies of such a program, whether gratis or for a fee, you must give the recipients all the rights that you have. You must make sure that they, too, receive or can get the source code. And you must show them these terms so they know their rights.

We protect your rights with two steps: (1) copyright the software, and (2) offer you this license which gives you legal permission to copy, distribute and/or modify the software.

Also, for each author's protection and ours, we want to make certain that everyone understands that there is no warranty for this free software. If the software is modified by someone else and passed on, we want its recipients to know that what they have is not the original, so that any problems introduced by others will not reflect on the original authors' reputations.

Finally, any free program is threatened constantly by software patents. We wish to avoid the danger that redistributors of a free program will individually obtain patent licenses, in effect making the program proprietary. To prevent this, we have made it clear that any patent must be licensed for everyone's free use or not licensed at all.

The precise terms and conditions for copying, distribution and modification follow.

F.2. GNU GENERAL PUBLIC LICENSE

TERMS AND CONDITIONS FOR COPYING, DISTRIBUTION AND MODIFICATION

0. This License applies to any program or other work which contains a notice placed by the copyright holder saying it may be distributed under the terms of this General Public License. The "Program", below, refers to any such program or work, and a "work based on the Program" means either the Program or any derivative work under copyright law: that is to say, a work containing the Program or a portion of it, either verbatim or with modifications and/or translated into another language. (Hereinafter, translation is included without limitation in the term "modification".) Each licensee is addressed as "you".

Activities other than copying, distribution and modification are not covered by this License; they are outside its scope. The act of running the Program is not restricted, and the output from the Program is covered only if its contents constitute a work based on the Program (independent of having been made by running the Program). Whether that is true depends on what the Program does.

1. You may copy and distribute verbatim copies of the Program's source code as you receive it, in any medium, provided that you conspicuously and appropriately publish on each copy an appropriate copyright notice and disclaimer of warranty; keep intact all the notices that refer to this License and to the absence of any warranty; and give any other recipients of the Program a copy of this License along with the Program.

You may charge a fee for the physical act of transferring a copy, and you may at your option offer warranty protection in exchange for a fee.

2. You may modify your copy or copies of the Program or any portion of it, thus forming a work based on the Program, and copy and distribute such modifications or work under the terms of Section 1 above, provided that you also meet all of these conditions:

   a. You must cause the modified files to carry prominent notices stating that you changed the files and the date of any change.

b. You must cause any work that you distribute or publish, that in whole or in part contains or is derived from the Program or any part thereof, to be licensed as a whole at no charge to all third parties under the terms of this License.

c. If the modified program normally reads commands interactively when run, you must cause it, when started running for such interactive use in the most ordinary way, to print or display an announcement including an appropriate copyright notice and a notice that there is no warranty (or else, saying that you provide a warranty) and that users may redistribute the program under these conditions, and telling the user how to view a copy of this License. (Exception: if the Program itself is interactive but does not normally print such an announcement, your work based on the Program is not required to print an announcement.)

These requirements apply to the modified work as a whole. If identifiable sections of that work are not derived from the Program, and can be reasonably considered independent and separate works in themselves, then this License, and its terms, do not apply to those sections when you distribute them as separate works. But when you distribute the same sections as part of a whole which is a work based on the Program, the distribution of the whole must be on the terms of this License, whose permissions for other licensees extend to the entire whole, and thus to each and every part regardless of who wrote it.

Thus, it is not the intent of this section to claim rights or contest your rights to work written entirely by you; rather, the intent is to exercise the right to control the distribution of derivative or collective works based on the Program.

In addition, mere aggregation of another work not based on the Program with the Program (or with a work based on the Program) on a volume of a storage or distribution medium does not bring the other work under the scope of this License.

3. You may copy and distribute the Program (or a work based on it, under Section 2) in object code or executable form under the terms of Sections 1 and 2 above provided that you also do one of the following:

a. Accompany it with the complete corresponding machine-readable source code, which must be distributed under the terms of Sections 1 and 2 above on a medium customarily used for software interchange; or,

b. Accompany it with a written offer, valid for at least three years, to give any third party, for a charge no more than your cost of physically performing source distribution, a complete machine-readable copy of the corresponding source code, to be distributed under the terms of Sections 1 and 2 above on a medium customarily used for software interchange; or,

c. Accompany it with the information you received as to the offer to distribute corresponding source code. (This alternative is allowed only for noncommercial distribution and only if you received the program in object code or executable form with such an offer, in accord with Subsection b above.)

The source code for a work means the preferred form of the work for making modifications to it. For an executable work, complete source code means all the source code for all modules it contains, plus any associated interface definition files, plus the scripts used to control compilation and installation of the executable. However, as a special exception, the source code distributed need not include anything that is normally distributed (in either source or binary form) with the major components (compiler, kernel, and so on) of the operating system on which the executable runs, unless that component itself accompanies the executable.

If distribution of executable or object code is made by offering access to copy from a designated place, then offering equivalent access to copy the source code from the same place counts as distribution of the source code, even though third parties are not compelled to copy the source along with the object code.

4. You may not copy, modify, sublicense, or distribute the Program except as expressly provided under this License. Any attempt otherwise to copy, modify, sublicense or distribute the Program is void, and will automatically terminate your rights under this License. However, parties who have received copies, or rights, from you under this License will not have their licenses terminated so long as such parties remain in full compliance.

5. You are not required to accept this License, since you have not signed it. However, nothing else grants you permission to modify or distribute the Program or its derivative works. These actions are prohibited by law if you do not accept this License. Therefore, by modifying or distributing the Program (or any work based on the Program), you indicate your acceptance of this License to do so, and all its terms and conditions for copying, distributing or modifying the Program or works based on it.

6. Each time you redistribute the Program (or any work based on the Program), the recipient automatically receives a license from the original licensor to copy, distribute or modify the Program subject to these terms and conditions. You may not impose any further restrictions on the recipients' exercise of the rights granted herein. You are not responsible for enforcing compliance by third parties to this License.

7. If, as a consequence of a court judgment or allegation of patent infringement or for any other reason (not limited to patent issues), conditions are imposed on you (whether by court order, agreement or otherwise) that contradict the conditions of this License, they do not excuse you from the conditions of this License. If you cannot distribute so as to satisfy simultaneously your obligations under this License and any other pertinent obligations, then as a consequence you may not distribute the Program at all. For example, if a patent license would not permit royalty-free redistribution of the Program by all those who receive copies directly or indirectly through you, then the only way you could satisfy both it and this License would be to refrain entirely from distribution of the Program.

If any portion of this section is held invalid or unenforceable under any particular circumstance, the balance of the section is intended to apply and the section as a whole is intended to apply in other circumstances.

It is not the purpose of this section to induce you to infringe any patents or other property right claims or to contest validity of any such claims; this section has the sole purpose of protecting the integrity of the free software distribution system, which is implemented by public license practices. Many people have made generous contributions to the wide range of software distributed through that system in reliance on consistent application of that system; it is up to the author/donor to decide if he or she is willing to distribute software through any other system and a licensee cannot impose that choice.

This section is intended to make thoroughly clear what is believed to be a consequence of the rest of this License.

8. If the distribution and/or use of the Program is restricted in certain countries either by patents or by copyrighted interfaces, the original copyright holder who places the Program under this License may add an explicit geographical distribution limitation excluding those countries, so that distribution is permitted only in or among countries not thus excluded. In such case, this License incorporates the limitation as if written in the body of this License.

9. The Free Software Foundation may publish revised and/or new versions of the General Public License from time to time. Such new versions will be similar in spirit to the present version, but may differ in detail to address new problems or concerns. Each version is given a distinguishing version number. If the Program specifies a version number of this License which applies to it and "any later version", you have the option of following the terms and conditions either of that version or of any later version published by the Free Software Foundation. If the Program does not specify a version number of this License, you may choose any version ever published by the Free Software Foundation.

10. If you wish to incorporate parts of the Program into other free programs whose distribution conditions are different, write to the author to ask for permission. For software which is copyrighted by the Free Software Foundation, write to the Free Software Foundation; we sometimes make exceptions for this. Our decision will be guided by the two goals of preserving the free status of all derivatives of our free software and of promoting the sharing and reuse of software generally.

NO WARRANTY

11. BECAUSE THE PROGRAM IS LICENSED FREE OF CHARGE, THERE IS NO WARRANTY FOR THE PROGRAM, TO THE EXTENT PERMITTED BY APPLICABLE

Installation Guide

LAW. EXCEPT WHEN OTHERWISE STATED IN WRITING THE COPYRIGHT HOLDERS AND/OR OTHER PARTIES PROVIDE THE PROGRAM "AS IS" WITHOUT WARRANTY OF ANY KIND, EITHER EXPRESSED OR IMPLIED, INCLUDING, BUT NOT LIMITED TO, THE IMPLIED WARRANTIES OF MERCHANTABILITY AND FITNESS FOR A PARTICULAR PURPOSE. THE ENTIRE RISK AS TO THE QUALITY AND PERFORMANCE OF THE PROGRAM IS WITH YOU. SHOULD THE PROGRAM PROVE DEFECTIVE, YOU ASSUME THE COST OF ALL NECESSARY SERVICING, REPAIR OR CORRECTION.

12. IN NO EVENT UNLESS REQUIRED BY APPLICABLE LAW OR AGREED TO IN WRITING WILL AND COPYRIGHT HOLDER, OR ANY OTHER PARTY WHO MAY MODIFY AND/OR REDISTRIBUTE THE PROGRAM AS PERMITTED ABOVE, BE LIABLE TO YOU FOR DAMAGES, INCLUDING ANY GENERAL, SPECIAL, INCIDENTAL OR CONSEQUENTIAL DAMAGES ARISING OUT OF THE USE OR INABILITY TO USE THE PROGRAM (INCLUDING BUT NOT LIMITED TO LOSS OF DATA OR DATA BEING RENDERED INACCURATE OR LOSSES SUSTAINED BY YOU OR THIRD PARTIES OR A FAILURE OF THE PROGRAM TO OPERATE WITH ANY OTHER PROGRAMS), EVEN IF SUCH HOLDER OR OTHER PARTY HAS BEEN ADVISED OF THE POSSIBILITY OF SUCH DAMAGES.

END OF TERMS AND CONDITIONS

F.3. How to Apply These Terms to Your New Programs

If you develop a new program, and you want it to be of the greatest possible use to the public, the best way to achieve this is to make it free software which everyone can redistribute and change under these terms.

To do so, attach the following notices to the program. It is safest to attach them to the start of each source file to most effectively convey the exclusion of warranty; and each file should have at least the "copyright" line and a pointer to where the full notice is found.

```
one line to give the program's name and a brief idea of what it does.
Copyright (C) year  name of author

This program is free software; you can redistribute it and/or
modify it under the terms of the GNU General Public License
as published by the Free Software Foundation; either version 2
of the License, or (at your option) any later version.

This program is distributed in the hope that it will be useful,
but WITHOUT ANY WARRANTY; without even the implied warranty of
MERCHANTABILITY OR FITNESS FOR A PARTICULAR PURPOSE. See the
GNU General Public License for more details.

You should have received a copy of the GNU General Public License
```

Ubuntu 9.10

```
along with this program; if not, write to the Free Software
Foundation, Inc., 51 Franklin Street, Fifth Floor, Boston, MA  02110-1301, USA.
```

Also add information on how to contact you by electronic and paper mail.

If the program is interactive, make it output a short notice like this when it starts in an interactive mode:

```
Gnomovision version 69, Copyright (C) year name of author
Gnomovision comes with absolutely no warranty; for details
type `show w'. This is free software, and you are welcome
to redistribute it under certain conditions; type `show c'
for details.
```

The hypothetical commands `show w' and `show c' should show the appropriate parts of the General Public License. Of course, the commands you use may be called something other than `show w' and `show c'; they could even be mouse-clicks or menu items — whatever suits your program.

You should also get your employer (if you work as a programmer) or your school, if any, to sign a "copyright disclaimer" for the program, if necessary. Here is a sample; alter the names:

```
Yoyodyne, Inc., hereby disclaims all copyright interest in the
program `Gnomovision' (which makes passes at compilers) written
by James Hacker.

signature of Ty Coon, 1 April 1989
Ty Coon, President of Vice
```

This General Public License does not permit incorporating your program into proprietary programs. If your program is a subroutine library, you may consider it more useful to permit linking proprietary applications with the library. If this is what you want to do, use the GNU Lesser General Public License instead of this License.

Ubuntu 9.10
Official Documentation Collection

Title	Author	Edition	ISBN-10	ISBN-13
Ubuntu 9.10 Installation Guide	Ubuntu Documentation Project	paperback	1-59682-171-X	978-1-59682-171-2
		eBook (pdf)	1-59682-175-2	978-1-59682-175-0
Ubuntu 9.10 Desktop Guide	Ubuntu Documentation Project	paperback	1-59682-172-8	978-1-59682-172-9
		eBook (pdf)	1-59682-176-0	978-1-59682-176-7
Ubuntu 9.10 Server Guide	Ubuntu Documentation Project	paperback	1-59682-173-6	978-1-59682-173-6
		eBook (pdf)	1-59682-177-9	978-1-59682-177-4
Ubuntu 9.10 Packaging Guide	Ubuntu Documentation Project	paperback	1-59682-174-4	978-1-59682-174-3
		eBook (pdf)	1-59682-178-7	978-1-59682-178-1
http://www.linbrary.com				